APOSTOLIC EXHORTATION

FAMILIARIS CONSORTIO

OF HIS HOLINESS

POPE JOHN PAUL II

TO THE EPISCOPATE
TO THE CLERGY AND TO THE FAITHFUL
OF THE WHOLE CATHOLIC CHURCH
REGARDING THE ROLE
OF THE CHRISTIAN FAMILY
IN THE MODERN WORLD

First published 1981 by the
Incorporated Catholic Truth Society
38–40 Eccleston Square
London SW1V 1PD

ISBN 0 85183 469 8

Translation: Vatican Polyglot Press

Printed by Tee & Whiten (Lincoln's Inn Press Ltd) Standard House,
Bonhill Street, London EC2A 4DA

INTRODUCTION

1.   THE FAMILY in the modern world, as
much as and perhaps more than any
other institution, has been beset by the many
profound and rapid changes that have affected
society and culture.   Many families are living
this situation in fidelity to those values that
constitute the foundation of the institution of the
family. Others have become uncertain and bewil-
dered over their role or even doubtful and
almost unaware of the ultimate meaning ·and
truth of conjugal and family life. Finally, there
are others who are hindered by various situations
of injustice in the realization of their fundamental
rights.

Knowing that marriage and the family
constitute one of the most precious of human
values, the Church wishes to speak and offer her
help to those who are already aware of the value
of marriage and the family and seek to live it
faithfully, to those who are uncertain and anxious
and searching for the truth, and to those who
are unjustly impeded from living freely their

family lives. Supporting the first, illuminating the second and assisting the others, the Church offers her services to every person who wonders about the destiny of marriage and the family.[1]

In a particular way the Church addresses the young, who are beginning their journey towards marriage and family life, for the purpose of presenting them with new horizons, helping them to discover the beauty and grandeur of the vocation to love and the service of life.

The Synod of 1980 in continuity with preceding Synods

2. A sign of this profound interest of the Church in the family was the last Synod of Bishops, held in Rome from 26 September to 25 October 1980. This was a natural continuation of the two preceding Synods: [2] the Christian family, in fact, is the first community called to announce the Gospel to the human person during growth and to bring him or her, through a progressive education and catechesis, to full human and Christian maturity.

Furthermore, the recent Synod is logically connected in some way as well with that on the ministerial priesthood and on justice in the modern world. In fact, as an educating com-

[1] Cf. Second Vatican Ecumenical Council, Pastoral Constitution on the Church in the Modern World *Gaudium et Spes*, 52.
[2] Cf. John Paul II, Homily for the Opening of the Sixth Synod of Bishops (26 September 1980), 2: *AAS* 72 (1980), 1008.

4

munity, the family must help man to discern his own vocation and to accept responsibility in the search for greater justice, educating him from the beginning in interpersonal relationships, rich in justice and in love.

At the close of their assembly, the Synod Fathers presented me with a long list of proposals in which they had gathered the fruits of their reflections, which had matured over intense days of work, and they asked me unanimously to be a spokesman before humanity of the Church's lively care for the family and to give suitable indications for renewed pastoral effort in this fundamental sector of the life of man and of the Church.

As I fulfil that mission with this Exhortation, thus actuating in a particular matter the apostolic ministry with which I am entrusted, I wish to thank all the members of the Synod for the very valuable contribution of teaching and experience that they made, especially through the *Propositiones,* the text of which I am entrusting to the Pontifical Council for the Family with instructions to study it so as to bring out every aspect of its rich content.

The precious value of marriage and of the family

3. Illuminated by the faith that gives her an understanding of all the truth concerning the great value of marriage and the family and their

deepest meaning, the Church once again feels the pressing need to proclaim the Gospel, that is the "good news", to all people without exception, in particular to all those who are called to marriage and are preparing for it, to all married couples and parents in the world.

The Church is deeply convinced that only by the acceptance of the Gospel are the hopes that man legitimately places in marriage and in the family capable of being fulfilled.

Willed by God in the very act of creation,[3] marriage and the family are interiorly ordained to fulfilment in Christ[4] and have need of his graces in order to be healed from the wounds of sin[5] and restored to their "beginning",[6] that is, to full understanding and the full realization of God's plan.

At a moment of history in which the family is the object of numerous forces that seek to destroy it or in some way to deform it, and aware that the well-being of society and her own good are intimately tied to the good of the family,[7] the Church perceives in a more urgent and compelling way her mission of proclaiming

[3] Cf. *Gen* 1-2.

[4] Cf. *Eph* 5.

[5] Cf. Second Vatican Ecumenical Council, Pastoral Constitution on the Church in the Modern World *Gaudium et Spes*, 47; Pope John Paul II, Letter *Appropinquat Iam* (15 August 1980), 1: *AAS* 72 (1980), 791.

[6] Cf. *Mt* 19:4.

[7] Cf. Second Vatican Ecumenical Council, Pastoral Constitution on the Church in the Modern World *Gaudium et Spes*, 47.

to all people the plan of God for marriage and the family, ensuring their full vitality and human and Christian development, and thus contributing to the renewal of society and of the People of God.

PART ONE

BRIGHT SPOTS AND SHADOWS
FOR THE FAMILY TODAY

**The need to understand
the situation**

4.   Since God's plan for marriage and the family touches men and women in the concreteness of their daily existence in specific social and cultural situations, the Church ought to apply herself to understanding the situations within which marriage and the family are lived today, in order to fulfil her task of serving.[8]

This understanding is, therefore, an inescapable requirement of the work of evangelization. It is, in fact, to the families of our times that the Church must bring the unchangeable and ever new Gospel of Jesus Christ, just as it is the families involved in the present conditions of the world that are called to accept and to live the plan of God that pertains to them. Moreover, the call and demands of the Spirit resound in the very events of history, and so the Church

[8] Cf. John Paul II, Address to the Council of the General Secretariat of the Synod of Bishops (23 February 1980): *Insegnamenti di Giovanni Paolo II*, III, 1 (1980), 472-476.

can also be guided to a more profound understanding of the inexhaustible mystery of marriage and the family by the circumstances, the questions and the anxieties and hopes of the young people, married couples and parents of today.[9]

To this ought to be added a further reflection of particular importance at the present time. Not infrequently ideas and solutions which are very appealing, but which obscure in varying degrees the truth and the dignity of the human person, are offered to the men and women of today, in their sincere and deep search for a response to the important daily problems that affect their married and family life. These views are often supported by the powerful and pervasive organization of the means of social communication, which subtly endanger freedom and the capacity for objective judgment.

Many are already aware of this danger to the human person and are working for the truth. The Church, with her evangelical discernment, joins with them, offering her own service to the truth, to freedom and to the dignity of every man and every woman.

Evangelical discernment

5.   The discernment effected by the Church becomes the offering of an orientation in order that the entire truth and the full dignity of marriage and the family may be preserved and realized.

[9] Cf. Second Vatican Ecumenical Council, Pastoral Constitution on the Church in the Modern World *Gaudium et Spes*, 4.

This discernment is accomplished through the sense of faith,[10] which is a gift that the Spirit gives to all the faithful,[11] and is therefore the work of the whole Church according to the diversity of the various gifts and charisms that, together with and according to the responsibility proper to each one, work together for a more profound understanding and activation of the word of God. The Church, therefore, does not accomplish this discernment only through the Pastors, who teach in the name and with the power of Christ, but also through the laity: Christ "made them his witnesses and gave them understanding of the faith and the grace of speech (cf. *Acts* 2:17-18; *Rev* 19:10), so that the power of the Gospel might shine forth in their daily social and family life".[12] The laity, moreover, by reason of their particular vocation have the specific role of interpreting the history of the world in the light of Christ, in as much as they are called to illuminate and organize temporal realities according to the plan of God, Creator and Redeemer.

The "supernatural sense of faith"[13] however does not consist solely or necessarily in the consensus of the faithful. Following Christ, the

---

[10] Cf. Second Vatican Ecumenical Council, Dogmatic Constitution on the Church *Lumen Gentium,* 12.

[11] Cf. *1 Jn* 2:20.

[12] Second Vatican Ecumenical Council, Dogmatic Constitution on the Church *Lumen Gentium,* 35.

[13] Cf. Second Vatican Ecumenical Council, Dogmatic Constitution on the Church *Lumen Gentium,* 12; Sacred Congregation for the Doctrine of the Faith, Declaration *Mysterium Ecclesiae,* 2: *AAS* 65 (1973), 398-400.

Church seeks the truth, which is not always the same as the majority opinion. She listens to conscience and not to power, and in this way she defends the poor and the downtrodden. The Church values sociological and statistical research, when it proves helpful in understanding the historical context in which pastoral action has to be developed and when it leads to a better understanding of the truth. Such research alone, however, is not to be considered in itself an expression of the sense of faith.

Because it is the task of the apostolic ministry to ensure that the Church remains in the truth of Christ and to lead her ever more deeply into that truth, the Pastors must promote the sense of the faith in all the faithful, examine and authoritatively judge the genuineness of its expressions, and educate the faithful in an ever more mature evangelical discernment.[14]

Christian spouses and parents can and should offer their unique and irreplaceable contribution to the elaboration of an authentic evangelical discernment in the various situations and cultures in which men and women live their marriage and their family life. They are qualified for this role by their charism or specific gift, the gift of the sacrament of matrimony.[15]

[14] Cf. Second Vatican Ecumenical Council, Dogmatic Constitution on the Church *Lumen Gentium,* 12; Dogmatic Constitution on Divine Revelation *Dei Verbum,* 10.

[15] Cf. John Paul II, Homily for the opening of the Sixth Synod of Bishops (26 September 1980), 3: *AAS* 72 (1980), 1008.

6.   The situation in which the family finds itself presents positive and negative aspects: the first are a sign of the salvation of Christ operating in the world; the second, a sign of the refusal that man gives to the love of God.

On the one hand, in fact, there is a more lively awareness of personal freedom and greater attention to the quality of interpersonal relationships in marriage, to promoting the dignity of women, to responsible procreation, to the education of children. There is also an awareness of the need for the development of interfamily relationships, for reciprocal spiritual and material assistance, the rediscovery of the ecclesial mission proper to the family and its responsibility for the building of a more just society. On the other hand, however, signs are not lacking of a disturbing degradation of some fundamental values: a mistaken theoretical and practical concept of the independence of the spouses in relation to each other; serious misconceptions regarding the relationship of authority between parents and children; the concrete difficulties that the family itself experiences in the transmission of values; the growing number of divorces; the scourge of abortion; the ever more frequent recourse to sterilization; the appearance of a truly contraceptive mentality.

At the root of these negative phenomena there

frequently lies a corruption of the idea and the experience of freedom, conceived not as a capacity for realizing the truth of God's plan for marriage and the family, but as an autonomous power of self-affirmation, often against others, for one's own selfish well-being.

Worthy of our attention also is the fact that, in the countries of the so-called Third World, families often lack both the means necessary for survival, such as food, work, housing and medicine, and the most elementary freedoms. In the richer countries, on the contrary, excessive prosperity and the consumer mentality, paradoxically joined to a certain anguish and uncertainty about the future, deprive married couples of the generosity and courage needed for raising up new human life: thus life is often perceived not as a blessing, but as a danger from which to defend oneself.

The historical situation in which the family lives therefore appears as an interplay of light and darkness.

This shows that history is not simply a fixed progression towards what is better, but rather an event of freedom, and even a struggle between freedoms that are in mutual conflict, that is, according to the well-known expression of Saint Augustine, a conflict between two loves: the love of God to the point of disregarding self, and the love of self to the point of disregarding God.[16]

---

[16] Cf. Saint Augustine, *De Civitate Dei,* XIV, 28: *CSEL* 40, II, 56-57.

It follows that only an education for love rooted in faith can lead to the capacity of interpreting "the signs of the times", which are the historical expression of this twofold love.

The influence of circumstances on the consciences of the faithful

7.   Living in such a world, under the pressures coming above all from the mass media, the faithful do not always remain immune from the obscuring of certain fundamental values, nor set themselves up as the critical conscience of family culture and as active agents in the building of an authentic family humanism.

Among the more troubling signs of this phenomenon, the Synod Fathers stressed the following, in particular: the spread of divorce and of recourse to a new union, even on the part of the faithful; the acceptance of purely civil marriage in contradiction to the vocation of the baptized to "be married in the Lord"; the celebration of the marriage sacrament without living faith, but for other motives; the rejection of the moral norms that guide and promote the human and Christian exercise of sexuality in marriage.

Our age needs wisdom

8.   The whole Church is obliged to a deep reflection and commitment, so that the new culture now emerging may be evangelized in depth, true

values acknowledged, the rights of men and women defended, and justice promoted in the very structures of society. In this way the "new humanism" will not distract people from their relationship with God, but will lead them to it more fully.

Science and its technical applications offer new and immense possibilities in the construction of such a humanism. Still, as a consequence of political choices that decide the direction of research and its applications, science is often used against its original purpose, which is the advancement of the human person.

It becomes necessary, therefore, on the part of all, to recover an awareness of the primacy of moral values, which are the values of the human person as such. The great task that has to be faced today for the renewal of society is that of recapturing the ultimate meaning of life and its fundamental values. Only an awareness of the primacy of these values enables man to use the immense possibilities given him by science in such a way as to bring about the true advancement of the human person in his or her whole truth, in his or her freedom and dignity. Science is called to ally itself with wisdom.

The following words of the Second Vatican Council can therefore be applied to the problems of the family: "Our era needs such wisdom more than bygone ages if the discoveries made by man are to be further humanized. For the future of the world stands in peril unless wiser people are forthcoming".[17]

The education of the moral conscience, which makes every human being capable of judging and of discerning the proper ways to achieve self-realization according to his or her original truth, thus becomes a pressing requirement that cannot be renounced.

Modern culture must be led to a more profoundly restored covenant with divine Wisdom. Every man is given a share of such Wisdom through the creating action of God. And it is only in faithfulness to this covenant that the families of today will be in a position to influence positively the building of a more just and fraternal world.

Gradualness and conversion

9. To the injustice originating from sin —which has profoundly penetrated the structures of today's world— and often hindering the family's full realization of itself and of its fundamental rights, we must all set ourselves in opposition through a conversion of mind and heart, following Christ Crucified by denying our own selfishness: such a conversion cannot fail to have a beneficial and renewing influence even on the structures of society.

What is needed is a continuous, permanent

[17] Pastoral Constitution on the Church in the Modern World *Gaudium et Spes*, 15.

conversion which, while requiring an interior detachment from every evil and an adherence to good in its fullness, is brought about concretely in steps which lead us ever forward. Thus a dynamic process develops, one which advances gradually with the progressive integration of the gifts of God and the demands of his definitive and absolute love in the entire personal and social life of man. Therefore an educational growth process is necessary, in order that individual believers, families and peoples, even civilization itself, by beginning from what they have already received of the mystery of Christ, may patiently be led forward, arriving at a richer understanding and a fuller integration of this mystery in their lives.

Inculturation

10.   In conformity with her constant tradition, the Church receives from the various cultures everything that is able to express better the unsearchable riches of Christ.[18] Only with the help of all the cultures will it be possible for these riches to be manifested ever more clearly, and for the Church to progress towards a daily more complete and profound awareness of the truth, which has already been given to her in its entirety by the Lord.

[18] Cf. *Eph* 3:8; Second Vatican Ecumenical Council, *Gaudium et Spes*, 44; Decree on the Church's Missionary Activity *Ad Gentes*, 15, 22.

Holding fast to the two principles of the compatibility with the Gospel of the various cultures to be taken up and of communion with the universal Church, there must be further study, particularly by the Episcopal Conferences and the appropriate departments of the Roman Curia, and greater pastoral diligence so that this "inculturation" of the Christian faith may come about ever more extensively, in the context of marriage and the family as well as in other fields.

It is by means of "inculturation" that one proceeds towards the full restoration of the covenant with the Wisdom of God, which is Christ himself. The whole Church will be enriched also by the cultures which, though lacking technology, abound in human wisdom and are enlivened by profound moral values.

So that the goal of this journey might be clear and consequently the way plainly indicated, the Synod was right to begin by considering in depth the original design of God for marriage and the family: it "went back to the beginning", in deference to the teaching of Christ.[19]

[19] Cf. *Mt* 19:4-6.

THE PLAN OF GOD
FOR MARRIAGE AND THE FAMILY

**Man, the image
of the God who is love**

11.   God created man in his own image and
likeness: [20] calling him to existence *through love,*
he called him at the same time *for love.*

God is love [21] and in himself he lives a
mystery of personal loving communion. Creating the human race in his own image and continually keeping it in being, God inscribed in the
humanity of man and woman the vocation, and
thus the capacity and responsibility, of love and
communion.[22] Love is therefore the fundamental
and innate vocation of every human being.

As an incarnate spirit, that is a soul which
expresses itself in a body and a body informed
by an immortal spirit, man is called to love in
his unified totality. Love includes the human

[20] Cf. *Gen* 1:26-27.
[21] *1 Jn* 4:8.
[22] Cf. Second Vatican Ecumenical Council, Pastoral Constitution on the Church in the Modern World *Gaudium et Spes,* 12.

19

body, and the body is made a sharer in spiritual love.

Christian revelation recognizes two specific ways of realizing the vocation of the human person, in its entirety, to love: marriage and virginity or celibacy. Either one is, in its own proper form, an actuation of the most profound truth of man, of his being "created in the image of God".

Consequently, sexuality, by means of which man and woman give themselves to one another through the acts which are proper and exclusive to spouses, is by no means something purely biological, but concerns the innermost being of the human person as such. It is realized in a truly human way only if it is an integral part of the love by which a man and a woman commit themselves totally to one another until death. The total physical self-giving would be a lie if it were not the sign and fruit of a total personal self-giving, in which the whole person, including the temporal dimension, is present: if the person were to withhold something or reserve the possibility of deciding otherwise in the future, by this very fact he or she would not be giving totally.

This totality which is required by conjugal love also corresponds to the demands of responsible fertility. This fertility is directed to the generation of a human being, and so by its nature it surpasses the purely biological order and involves a whole series of personal values. For the harmonious growth of these values a per-severing and unified contribution by both parents is necessary.

The only "place" in which this self-giving in its whole truth is made possible is marriage, the covenant of conjugal love freely and consciously chosen, whereby man and woman accept the intimate community of life and love willed by God himself,[23] which only in this light manifests its true meaning. The institution of marriage is not an undue interference by society or authority, nor the extrinsic imposition of a form. Rather it is an interior requirement of the covenant of conjugal love which is publicly affirmed as unique and exclusive, in order to live in complete fidelity to the plan of God, the Creator. A person's freedom, far from being restricted by this fidelity, is secured against every form of subjectivism or relativism and is made a sharer in creative Wisdom.

Marriage and communion between God and people

12.   The communion of love between God and people, a fundamental part of the Revelation and faith experience of Israel, finds a meaningful expression in the marriage covenant which is established between a man and a woman.

For this reason the central word of Rev-

[23] Cf. *ibid.*, 48.

elation, "God loves his people", is likewise proclaimed through the living and concrete word whereby a man and a woman express their conjugal love. Their bond of love becomes the image and the symbol of the covenant which unites God and his people.[24] And the same sin which can harm the conjugal covenant becomes an image of the infidelity of the people to their God: idolatry is prostitution,[25] infidelity is adultery, disobedience to the law is abandonment of the spousal love of the Lord. But the infidelity of Israel does not destroy the eternal fidelity of the Lord, and therefore the ever faithful love of God is put forward as the model of the relations of faithful love which should exist between spouses.[26]

Jesus Christ, Bridegroom of the Church, and the sacrament of Matrimony

13.   The communion between God and his people finds its definitive fulfilment in Jesus Christ, the Bridegroom who loves and gives himself as the Saviour of humanity, uniting it to himself as his body.

He reveals the original truth of marriage, the truth of the "beginning",[27] and, freeing man from his hardness of heart, he makes man capable of realizing this truth in its entirety.

[24] Cf. e.g. *Hos* 2:21; *Jer* 3:6-13; *Is* 54.
[25] Cf. *Ezek* 16:25.
[26] Cf. *Hos* 3.
[27] Cf. *Gen* 2:24; *Mt* 19:5.

22

This revelation reaches its definitive fullness in the gift of love which the Word of God makes to humanity in assuming a human nature, and in the sacrifice which Jesus Christ makes of himself on the Cross for his bride, the Church. In this sacrifice there is entirely revealed that plan which God has imprinted on the humanity of man and woman since their creation; [28] the marriage of baptized persons thus becomes a real symbol of that new and eternal covenant sanctioned in the blood of Christ. The Spirit which the Lord pours forth gives a new heart, and renders man and woman capable of loving one another as Christ has loved us. Conjugal love reaches that fullness to which it is interiorly ordained, conjugal charity, which is the proper and specific way in which the spouses participate in and are called to live the very charity of Christ who gave himself on the Cross.

In a deservedly famous page, Tertullian has well expressed the greatness of this conjugal life in Christ and its beauty: "How can I ever express the happiness of the marriage that is joined together by the Church, strengthened by an offering, sealed by a blessing, announced by angels and ratified by the Father? ... How wonderful the bond between two believers, with a single hope, a single desire, a single observance, a single service! They are both brethren and both fellow-servants; there is no separation

[28] Cf. *Eph* 5:32-33.

between them in spirit or flesh; in fact they are truly two in one flesh, and where the flesh is one, one is the spirit".[29]

Receiving and meditating faithfully on the word of God, the Church has solemnly taught and continues to teach that the marriage of the baptized is one of the seven sacraments of the New Covenant.[30]

Indeed, by means of baptism, man and woman are definitively placed within the new and eternal covenant, in the spousal covenant of Christ with the Church. And it is because of this indestructible insertion that the intimate community of conjugal life and love, founded by the Creator,[31] is elevated and assumed into the spousal charity of Christ, sustained and enriched by his redeeming power.

By virtue of the sacramentality of their marriage, spouses are bound to one another in the most profoundly indissoluble manner. Their belonging to each other is the real representation, by means of the sacramental sign, of the very relationship of Christ with the Church.

Spouses are therefore the permanent reminder to the Church of what happened on the Cross; they are for one another and for the children

[29] Tertullian, *Ad Uxorem*, II, VIII, 6-8: *CCL*, I, 393.

[30] Cf. Ecumenical Council of Trent, Session XXIV, canon 1: I. D. Mansi, *Sacrorum Conciliorum Nova et Amplissima Collectio*, 33, 149-150.

[31] Cf. Second Vatican Ecumenical Council, Pastoral Constitution on the Church in the Modern World *Gaudium et Spes*, 48.

witnesses to the salvation in which the sacrament makes them sharers. Of this salvation event marriage, like every sacrament, is a memorial, actuation and prophecy: "As a memorial, the sacrament gives them the grace and duty of commemorating the great works of God and of bearing witness to them before their children. As actuation, it gives them the grace and duty of putting into practice in the present, towards each other and their children, the demands of a love which forgives and redeems. As prophecy, it gives them the grace and duty of living and bearing witness to the hope of the future encounter with Christ".[32]

Like each of the seven sacraments, so also marriage is a real symbol of the event of salvation, but in its own way. "The spouses participate in it as spouses, together, as a couple, so that the first and immediate effect of marriage (*res et sacramentum*) is not supernatural grace itself, but the Christian conjugal bond, a typically Christian communion of two persons because it represents the mystery of Christ's incarnation and the mystery of his covenant. The content of participation in Christ's life is also specific: conjugal love involves a totality, in which all the elements of the person enter—appeal of the body and instinct, power of feeling and affectivity, aspiration of the spirit and of will. It aims at a

---

[32] John Paul II, Address to the Delegates of the Centre de Liaison des Equipes de Recherche (3 November 1979), 3: *Insegnamenti di Giovanni Paolo II*, II, 2 (1979), 1038.

deeply personal unity, the unity that, beyond union in one flesh, leads to forming one heart and soul; it demands indissolubility and faithfulness in definitive mutual giving; and it is open to fertility (cf. *Humanae Vitae,* 9). In a word it is a question of the normal characteristics of all natural conjugal love, but with a new significance which not only purifies and strengthens them, but raises them to the extent of making them the expression of specifically Christian values ".[33]

Children, the precious gift of marriage

14. According to the plan of God, marriage is the foundation of the wider community of the family, since the very institution of marriage and conjugal love are ordained to the procreation and education of children, in whom they find their crowning.[34]

In its most profound reality, love is essentially a gift; and conjugal love, while leading the spouses to the reciprocal "knowledge" which makes them "one flesh",[35] does not end with the couple, because it makes them capable of the greatest possible gift, the gift by which they become cooperators with God for giving life to a new human person. Thus the couple, while

---

[33] *Ibid.,* 4: *loc. cit.,* 1032.
[34] Cf. Second Vatican Ecumenical Council, Pastoral Constitution on the Church in the Modern World *Gaudium et Spes,* 50.
[35] Cf. *Gen* 2:24.

giving themselves to one another, give not just themselves but also the reality of children, who are a living reflection of their love, a permanent sign of conjugal unity and a living and inseparable synthesis of their being a father and a mother.

When they become parents, spouses receive from God the gift of a new responsibility. Their parental love is called to become for the children the visible sign of the very love of God, "from whom every family in heaven and on earth is named".[36]

It must not be forgotten however that, even when procreation is not possible, conjugal life does not for this reason lose its value. Physical sterility in fact can be for spouses the occasion for other important services to the life of the human person, for example, adoption, various forms of educational work, and assistance to other families and to poor or handicapped children.

**The family,
a communion of persons**

15.   In matrimony and in the family a complex of interpersonal relationships is set up —married life, fatherhood and motherhood, filiation and fraternity—through which each human person is introduced into the "human family" and into the "family of God", which is the Church.

[36] *Eph* 3:15.

Christian marriage and the Christian family build up the Church: for in the family the human person is not only brought into being and progressively introduced by means of education into the human community, but by means of the rebirth of baptism and education in the faith the child is also introduced into God's family, which is the Church.

The human family, disunited by sin, is reconstituted in its unity by the redemptive power of the death and Resurrection of Christ.[37] Christian marriage, by participating in the salvific efficacy of this event, constitutes the natural setting in which the human person it introduced into the great family of the Church.

The commandment to grow and multiply, given to man and woman in the beginning, in this way reaches its whole truth and full realization.

The Church thus finds in the family, born from the sacrament, the cradle and the setting in which she can enter the human generations, and where these in their turn can enter the Church.

Marriage and virginity or celibacy

16.   Virginity or celibacy for the sake of the Kingdom of God not only does not contradict the dignity of marriage but presupposes it and

---

[37] Cf. Second Vatican Ecumenical Council, Pastoral Constitution on the Church in the Modern World *Gaudium et Spes,* 78.

confirms it. Marriage and virginity or celibacy are two ways of expressing and living the one mystery of the covenant of God with his people. When marriage is not esteemed, neither can consecrated virginity or celibacy exist; when human sexuality is not regarded as a great value given by the Creator, the renunciation of it for the sake of the Kingdom of Heaven loses its meaning.

Rightly indeed does Saint John Chrysostom say: "Whoever denigrates marriage also diminishes the glory of virginity. Whoever praises it makes virginity more admirable and resplendent. What appears good only in comparison with evil would not be particularly good. It is something better than what is admitted to be good that is the most excellent good".[38]

In virginity or celibacy, the human being is awaiting, also in a bodily way, the eschatological marriage of Christ with the Church, giving himself or herself completely to the Church in the hope that Christ may give himself to the Church in the full truth of eternal life. The celibate person thus anticipates in his or her flesh the new world of the future resurrection.[39]

By virtue of this witness, virginity or celibacy keeps alive in the Church a consciousness of the mystery of marriage and defends it from any reduction and impoverishment.

---

[38] Saint John Chrysostom, *Virginity*, X: *PG* 48: 540.
[39] Cf. *Mt* 22: 30.

Virginity or celibacy, by liberating the human heart in a unique way,[40] "so as to make it burn with greater love for God and all humanity",[41] bears witness that the Kingdom of God and his justice is that pearl of great price which is preferred to every other value no matter how great, and hence must be sought as the only definitive value. It is for this reason that the Church, throughout her history, has always defended the superiority of this charism to that of marriage, by reason of the wholly singular link which it has with the Kingdom of God.[42]

In spite of having renounced physical fecundity, the celibate person becomes spiritually fruitful, the father and mother of many, cooperating in the realization of the family according to God's plan.

Christian couples therefore have the right to expect from celibate persons a good example and a witness of fidelity to their vocation until death. Just as fidelity at times becomes difficult for married people and requires sacrifice, mortification and self-denial, the same can happen to celibate persons, and their fidelity, even in the trials that may occur, should strengthen the fidelity of married couples.[43]

[40] Cf. *1 Cor* 7:32-35.
[41] Second Vatican Ecumenical Council, Decree on Renewal of Religious Life *Perfectae Caritatis,* 12.
[42] Cf. Pius XII, Encyclical *Sacra Virginitas,* II: *AAS* 46 (1954), 174 ff.
[43] Cf. John Paul II, Letter *Novo Incipiente* (8 April 1979), 9: *AAS* 71 (1979), 410-411.

These reflections on virginity or celibacy can enlighten and help those who, for reasons independent of their own will, have been unable to marry and have then accepted their situation in a spirit of service.

PART THREE

THE ROLE OF THE CHRISTIAN FAMILY

Family, become what you are

17.   The family finds in the plan of God the Creator and Redeemer not only its *identity,* what it *is,* but also its *mission,* what it can and should *do.* The role that God calls the family to perform in history derives from what the family is; its role represents the dynamic and existential development of what it is.   Each family finds within itself a summons that cannot be ignored, and that specifies both its dignity and its responsibility: family, *become* what you *are.*

Accordingly, the family must go back to the "beginning" of God's creative act, if it is to attain self-knowledge and self-realization in accordance with the inner truth not only of what it is but also of what it does in history.   And since in God's plan it has been established as an "intimate community of life and love",[44] the

---

[44] Second Vatican Ecumenical Council, Pastoral Constitution on the Church in the Modern World *Gaudium et Spes,* 48.

family has the mission to become more and more what it is, that is to say, a community of life and love, in an effort that will find fulfilment, as will everything created and redeemed, in the Kingdom of God. Looking at it in such a way as to reach its very roots, we must say that the essence and role of the family are in the final analysis specified by love. Hence the family has *the mission to guard, reveal and communicate love,* and this is a living reflection of and a real sharing in God's love for humanity and the love of Christ the Lord for the Church his bride.

Every particular task of the family is an expression and concrete actuation of that fundamental mission. We must therefore go deeper into the unique riches of the family's mission and probe its contents, which are both manifold and unified.

Thus, with love as its point of departure and making constant reference to it, the recent Synod emphasized four general tasks for the family:

    1) forming a community of persons;

    2) serving life;

    3) participating in the development of society;

    4) sharing in the life and mission of the Church.

2 (2413)

**Love as the principle
and power of communion**

18.   The family, which is founded and given
life by love, is a community of persons: of husband and wife, of parents and children, of
relatives. Its first task is to live with fidelity the
reality of communion in a constant effort to
develop an authentic community of persons.

The inner principle of that task, its permanent
power and its final goal is love: without love
the family is not a community of persons and,
in the same way, *without love the family cannot
live, grow and perfect itself as a community of
persons*.   What I wrote in the Encyclical
Redemptor Hominis applies primarily and especially within the family as such: "Man cannot
live without love. He remains a being that is
incomprehensible for himself, his life is senseless,
if love is not revealed to him, if he does not
encounter love, if he does not experience it and
make it his own, if he does not participate
intimately in it ".[45]

The love between husband and wife and, in
a derivatory and broader way, the love between
members of the same family—between parents
and children, brothers and sisters and relatives
and members of the household—is given life and

[45] Encyclical *Redemptor Hominis*, 10: *AAS* 71 (1979), 274.

sustenance by an unceasing inner dynamism leading the family to ever deeper and more intense *communion*, which is the foundation and soul of the *community* of marriage and the family.

**The indivisible unity
of conjugal communion**

19. The first communion is the one which is established and which develops between husband and wife: by virtue of the covenant of married life, the man and woman "are no longer two but one flesh" [46] and they are called to grow continually in their communion through day-to-day fidelity to their marriage promise of total mutual self-giving.

This conjugal communion sinks its roots in the natural complementarity that exists between man and woman, and is nurtured through the personal willingness of the spouses to share their entire life-project, what they have and what they are: for this reason such communion is the fruit and the sign of a profoundly human need. But in the Lord Christ God takes up this human need, confirms it, purifies it and elevates it, leading it to perfection through the sacrament of Matrimony: the Holy Spirit who is poured out in the sacramental celebration offers Christian couples the gift of a new communion of love that is the living and real image of that unique unity which

[46] *Mt* 19:6; cf. *Gen* 2:24.

makes of the Church the indivisible Mystical Body of the Lord Jesus.

The gift of the Spirit is a commandment of life for Christian spouses and at the same time a stimulating impulse so that every day they may progress towards an ever richer union with each other on all levels—of the body, of the character, of the heart, of the intelligence and will, of the soul [47]—revealing in this way to the Church and to the world the new communion of love, given by the grace of Christ.

Such a communion is radically contradicted by polygamy: this, in fact, directly negates the plan of God which was revealed from the beginning, because it is contrary to the equal personal dignity of men and women who in matrimony give themselves with a love that is total and therefore unique and exclusive. As the Second Vatican Council writes: "Firmly established by the Lord, the unity of marriage will radiate from the equal personal dignity of husband and wife, a dignity acknowledged by mutual and total love".[48]

[47] Cf. John Paul II, Address to Married People at Kinshasa (3 May 1980), 4: *AAS* 72 (1980), 426-427.
[48] Pastoral Constitution on the Church in the Modern World *Gaudium et Spes,* 49; cf. John Paul II, Address to Married People at Kinshasa (3 May 1980), 4: *loc. cit.*

20.   Conjugal communion is characterized not only by its unity but also by its indissolubility: "As a mutual gift of two persons, this intimate union, as well as the good of children, imposes total fidelity on the spouses and argues for an unbreakable oneness between them".[49]

It is a fundamental duty of the Church to reaffirm strongly, as the Synod Fathers did, the doctrine of the indissolubility of marriage. To all those who, in our times, consider it too difficult, or indeed impossible, to be bound to one person for the whole of life, and to those caught up in a culture that rejects the indissolubility of marriage and openly mocks the commitment of spouses to fidelity, it is necessary to reconfirm the good news of the definitive nature of that conjugal love that has in Christ its foundation and strength.[50]

Being rooted in the personal and total self-giving of the couple, and being required by the good of the children, the indissolubility of marriage finds its ultimate truth in the plan that God has manifested in his revelation: he wills and he communicates the indissolubility of marriage as a fruit, a sign and a requirement of the absolutely faithful love that God has for man and that the Lord Jesus has for the Church.

[49] Second Vatican Ecumenical Council, Pastoral Constitution on the Church in the Modern World *Gaudium et Spes,* 48.
[50] Cf. *Eph* 5:25.

Christ renews the first plan that the Creator inscribed in the hearts of man and woman, and in the celebration of the sacrament of matrimony offers "a new heart": thus the couples are not only able to overcome "hardness of heart",[51] but also and above all they are able to share the full and definitive love of Christ, the new and eternal Covenant made flesh. Just as the Lord Jesus is the "faithful witness",[52] the "yes" of the promises of God[53] and thus the supreme realization of the unconditional faithfulness with which God loves his people, so Christian couples are called to participate truly in the irrevocable indissolubility that binds Christ to the Church his bride, loved by him to the end.[54]

The gift of the sacrament is at the same time a vocation and commandment for the Christian spouses, that they may remain faithful to each other forever, beyond every trial and difficulty, in generous obedience to the holy will of the Lord: "What therefore God has joined together, let not man put asunder".[55]

To bear witness to the inestimable value of the indissolubility and fidelity of marriage is one of the most precious and most urgent tasks of Christian couples in our time. So, with all my Brothers who participated in the Synod of Bishops, I praise and encourage those numerous

[51] *Mt* 19:8.
[52] *Rev* 3:14.
[53] Cf. *2 Cor* 1:20.
[54] Cf. *Jn* 13:1.
[55] *Mt* 19:6.

couples who, though encountering no small difficulty, preserve and develop the value of indissolubility: thus, in a humble and courageous manner, they perform the role committed to them of being in the world a "sign"—a small and precious sign, sometimes also subjected to temptation, but always renewed—of the unfailing fidelity with which God and Jesus Christ love each and every human being. But it is also proper to recognize the value of the witness of those spouses who, even when abandoned by their partner, with the strength of faith and of Christian hope have not entered a new union: these spouses too give an authentic witness to fidelity, of which the world today has a great need. For this reason they must be encouraged and helped by the pastors and the faithful of the Church.

The broader communion of the family

21. Conjugal communion constitutes the foundation on which is built the broader communion of the family, of parents and children, of brothers and sisters with each other, of relatives and other members of the household.

This communion is rooted in the natural bonds of flesh and blood, and grows to its specifically human perfection with the establishment and maturing of the still deeper and richer bonds of the spirit: the love that animates the interpersonal relationships of the different members of the family constitutes the interior strength that shapes and animates the family communion and community.

The Christian family is also called to experience a new and original communion which confirms and perfects natural and human communion. In fact the grace of Jesus Christ, "the first-born among many brethren",[56] is by its nature and interior dynamism "a grace of brotherhood", as Saint Thomas Aquinas calls it.[57] The Holy Spirit, who is poured forth in the celebration of the sacraments, is the living source and inexhaustible sustenance of the supernatural communion that gathers believers and links them with Christ and with each other in the unity of the Church of God. The Christian family constitutes a specific revelation and realization of ecclesial communion, and for this reason too it can and should be called "the domestic Church".[58]

All members of the family, each according to his or her own gift, have the grace and responsibility of building, day by day, the communion of persons, making the family "a school of deeper humanity": [59] this happens where there is care and love for the little ones, the sick, the aged; where there is mutual service every day;

---

[56] *Rom* 8:29.

[57] Saint Thomas Aquinas, *Summa Theologiae*, II-II, q. 14, art. 2, ad 4.

[58] Second Vatican Ecumenical Council, Dogmatic Constitution on the Church *Lumen Gentium,* 11; cf. Decree on the Apostolate of the Laity *Apostolicam Actuositatem,* 11.

[59] Second Vatican Ecumenical Council, Pastoral Constitution on the Church in the Modern World *Gaudium et Spes,* 52.

when there is a sharing of goods, of joys and of sorrows.

A fundamental opportunity for building such a communion is constituted by the educational exchange between parents and children,[60] in which each gives and receives. By means of love, respect and obedience towards their parents, children offer their specific and irreplaceable contribution to the construction of an authentically human and Christian family.[61] They will be aided in this if parents exercise their unrenounceable authority as a true and proper "ministry", that is, as a service to the human and Christian well-being of their children, and in particular as a service aimed at helping them acquire a truly responsible freedom, and if parents maintain a living awareness of the "gift" they continually receive from their children.

Family communion can only be preserved and perfected through a great spirit of sacrifice. It requires, in fact, a ready and generous openness of each and all to understanding, to forbearance, to pardon, to reconciliation. There is no family that does not know how selfishness, discord, tension and conflict violently attack and at times mortally wound its own communion: hence there arise the many and varied forms of division in family life. But, at the same time, every family is called by the God of peace to

[60] Cf. *Eph* 6:1-4; *Col* 3:20-21.
[61] Cf. Second Vatican Ecumenical Council, Pastoral Constitution on the Church in the Modern World *Gaudium et Spes*, 48.

41

have the joyous and renewing experience of "reconciliation", that is, communion reestablished, unity restored. In particular, participation in the sacrament of Reconciliation and in the banquet of the one Body of Christ offers to the Christian family the grace and the responsibility of overcoming every division and of moving towards the fullness of communion willed by God, responding in this way to the ardent desire of the Lord: "that they may be one".[62]

The rights and role of women

22.   In that it is, and ought always to become, a communion and community of persons, the family finds in love the source and the constant impetus for welcoming, respecting and promoting each one of its members in his or her lofty dignity as a person, that is, as a living image of God. As the Synod Fathers rightly stated, the moral criterion for the authenticity of conjugal and family relationships consists in fostering the dignity and vocation of the individual persons, who achieve their fullness by sincere self-giving.[63]

In this perspective the Synod devoted special attention to women, to their rights and role

---

[62] *Jn* 17:21.
[63] Cf. Second Vatican Ecumenical Council, Pastoral Constitution on the Church in the Modern World *Gaudium et Spes,* 24.

within the family and society. In the same perspective are also to be considered men as husbands and fathers, and likewise children and the elderly.

Above all it is important to underline the equal dignity and responsibility of women with men. This equality is realized in a unique manner in that reciprocal self-giving by each one to the other and by both to the children which is proper to marriage and the family. What human reason intuitively perceives and acknowledges is fully revealed by the word of God: the history of salvation, in fact, is a continuous and luminous testimony to the dignity of women.

In creating the human race "male and female",[64] God gives man and woman an equal personal dignity, endowing them with the inalienable rights and responsibilities proper to the human person. God then manifests the dignity of women in the highest form possible, by assuming human flesh from the Virgin Mary, whom the Church honours as the Mother of God, calling her the new Eve and presenting her as the model of redeemed woman. The sensitive respect of Jesus towards the women that he called to his following and his friendship, his appearing on Easter morning to a woman before the other disciples, the mission entrusted to women to carry the good news of the Resurrection to the Apostles—these are all signs that confirm the

[64] *Gen* 1:27.

special esteem of the Lord Jesus for women. The Apostle Paul will say: "In Christ Jesus you are all children of God through faith ... There is neither Jew nor Greek, there is neither slave nor free, there is neither male nor female; for you are all one in Christ Jesus".[65]

Women and society

23.   Without intending to deal with all the various aspects of the vast and complex theme of the relationships between women and society, and limiting these remarks to a few essential points, one cannot but observe that in the specific area of family life a widespread social and cultural tradition has considered women's role to be exclusively that of wife and mother, without adequate access to public functions, which have generally been reserved for men.

There is no doubt that the equal dignity and responsibility of men and women fully justifies women's access to public functions. On the other hand the true advancement of women requires that clear recognition be given to the value of their maternal and family role, by comparison with all other public roles and all other professions. Furthermore, these roles and professions should be harmoniously combined, if we wish the evolution of society and culture to be truly and fully human.

[65] *Gal* 3:26, 28.

This will come about more easily if, in accordance with the wishes expressed by the Synod, a renewed "theology of work" can shed light upon and study in depth the meaning of work in the Christian life and determine the fundamental bond between work and the family, and therefore the original and irreplaceable meaning of work in the home and in rearing children.[66] Therefore the Church can and should help modern society by tirelessly insisting that the work of women in the home be recognized and respected by all in its irreplaceable value. This is of particular importance in education: for possible discrimination between the different types of work and professions is eliminated at its very root once it is clear that all people, in every area, are working with equal rights and equal responsibilities. The image of God in man and in woman will thus be seen with added lustre.

While it must be recognized that women have the same right as men to perform various public functions, society must be structured in such a way that wives and mothers are *not in practice compelled* to work outside the home, and that their families can live and prosper in a dignified way even when they themselves devote their full time to their own family.

Furthermore, the mentality which honours

---

[66] Cf. John Paul II, Encyclical *Laborem Exercens*, 19: *AAS* 73 (1981), 625.

women more for their work outside the home than for their work within the family must be overcome. This requires that men should truly esteem and love women with total respect for their personal dignity, and that society should create and develop conditions favouring work in the home.

With due respect to the different vocations of men and women, the Church must in her own life promote as far as possible their equality of rights and dignity: and this for the good of all, the family, the Church and society.

But clearly all of this does not mean for women a renunciation of their femininity or an imitation of the male role, but the fullness of true feminine humanity which should be expressed in their activity, whether in the family or outside of it, without disregarding the differences of customs and cultures in this sphere.

Offences against women's dignity

24.   Unfortunately the Christian message about the dignity of women is contradicted by that persistent mentality which considers the human being not as a person but as a thing, as an object of trade, at the service of selfish interest and mere pleasure: the first victims of this mentality are women.

This mentality produces very bitter fruits, such as contempt for men and for women, slavery, oppression of the weak, pornography, prostitution —especially in an organized form—and all those various forms of discrimination that exist in the fields of education, employment, wages, etc.

Besides, many forms of degrading discrimination still persist today in a great part of our society that affect and seriously harm particular categories of women, as for example childless wives, widows, separated or divorced women, and unmarried mothers.

The Synod Fathers deplored these and other forms of discriminations as strongly as possible. I therefore ask that vigorous and incisive pastoral action be taken by all to overcome them definitively so that the image of God that shines in all human beings without exception may be fully respected.

Men as husbands and fathers

25. Within the conjugal and family communion-community, the man is called upon to live his gift and role as husband and father.

In his wife he sees the fulfilment of God's intention: "It is not good that the man should be alone; I will make him a helper fit for him",[67] and he makes his own the cry of Adam, the first husband: "This at last is bone of my bones and flesh of my flesh".[68]

[67] *Gen* 2:18.
[68] *Gen* 2:23.

Authentic conjugal love presupposes and requires that a man have a profound respect for the equal dignity of his wife: "You are not her master", writes Saint Ambrose, "but her husband; she was not given to you to be your slave, but your wife ... Reciprocate her attentiveness to you and be grateful to her for her love".[69] With his wife a man should live "a very special form of personal friendship".[70] As for the Christian, he is called upon to develop a new attitude of love, manifesting towards his wife a charity that is both gentle and strong like that which Christ has for the Church.[71]

Love for his wife as mother of their children and love for the children themselves are for the man the natural way of understanding and fulfilling his own fatherhood. Above all where social and cultural conditions so easily encourage a father to be less concerned with his family or at any rate less involved in the work of education, efforts must be made to restore socially the conviction that the place and task of the father in and for the family is of unique and irreplaceable importance.[72] As experience teaches, the absence of a father causes psychological and moral imbalance and notable difficulties in family relationships, as does, in contrary circumstances, the op-

[69] Saint Ambrose, *Exameron*, V, 7, 19: *CSEL* 32, I, 154.
[70] Paul VI, Encyclical *Humanae Vitae*, 9: *AAS* 60 (1968), 486.
[71] Cf. *Eph* 5:25.
[72] Cf. John Paul II, Homily to the faithful of Terni (19 March 1981), 3-5: *AAS* 73 (1981), 268-271.

pressive presence of a father, especially where there still prevails the phenomenon of "machismo", or a wrong superiority of male prerogatives which humiliates women and inhibits the development of healthy family relationships.

In revealing and in reliving on earth the very fatherhood of God,[73] a man is called upon to ensure the harmonious and united development of all the members of the family: he will perform this task by exercising generous responsibility for the life conceived under the heart of the mother, by a more solicitous commitment to education, a task he shares with his wife,[74] by work which is never a cause of division in the family but promotes its unity and stability, and by means of the witness he gives of an adult Christian life which effectively introduces the children into the living experience of Christ and the Church.

The rights of children

26.   In the family, which is a community of persons, special attention must be devoted to the children, by developing a profound esteem for their personal dignity, and a great respect and generous concern for their rights. This is true for every child, but it becomes all the more urgent the smaller the child is and the more it is in need of everything, when it is sick, suffering or handicapped.

[73] Cf. *Eph* 3:15.
[74] Cf. Second Vatican Ecumenical Council, Pastoral Constitution on the Church in the Modern World *Gaudium et Spes*, 52.

By fostering and exercising a tender and strong concern for every child that comes into this world, the Church fulfils a fundamental mission: for she is called upon to reveal and put forward anew in history the example and the commandment of Christ the Lord, who placed the child at the heart of the Kingdom of God: "Let the children come to me, and do not hinder them; for to such belongs the kingdom of heaven".[75]

I repeat once again what I said to the General Assembly of the United Nations on 2 October 1979: "I wish to express the joy that we all find in children, the springtime of life, the anticipation of the future history of each of our present earthly homelands. No country on earth, no political system can think of its own future otherwise than through the image of these new generations that will receive from their parents the manifold heritage of values, duties and aspirations of the nation to which they belong and of the whole human family. Concern for the child, even before birth, from the first moment of conception and then throughout the years of infancy and youth, is the primary and fundamental test of the relationship of one human being to another. And so, what better wish can I express for every nation and for the whole of mankind, and for all the children of the world than a better future in which respect for human rights will become

[75] *Lk* 18:16; cf. *Mt* 19:14; *Mk* 18:16.

a complete reality throughout the third millennium, which is drawing near".[76]

Acceptance, love, esteem, manysided and united material, emotional, educational and spiritual concern for every child that comes into this world should always constitute a distinctive, essential characteristic of all Christians, in particular of the Christian family: thus children, while they are able to grow "in wisdom and in stature, and in favour with God and man",[77] offer their own precious contribution to building up the family community and even to the sanctification of their parents.[78]

The elderly in the family

27.   There are cultures which manifest a unique veneration and great love for the elderly: far from being outcasts from the family or merely tolerated as a useless burden, they continue to be present and to take an active and responsible part in family life, though having to respect the autonomy of the new family; above all they carry out the important mission of being a witness to the past and a source of wisdom for the young and for the future.

[76] John Paul II, Address to the General Assembly of the United Nations (2 October 1979), 21: *AAS* 71 (1979), 1159.
[77] *Lk* 2:52.
[78] Cf. Second Vatican Ecumenical Council, Pastoral Constitution on the Church in the Modern World *Gaudium et Spes*, 48.

Other cultures, however, especially in the wake of disordered industrial and urban development, have both in the past and in the present set the elderly aside in unacceptable ways. This causes acute suffering to them and spiritually impoverishes many families.

The pastoral activity of the Church must help everyone to discover and to make good use of the role of the elderly within the civil and ecclesial community, in particular within the family. In fact, "the life of the aging helps to clarify a scale of human values; it shows the continuity of generations and marvellously demonstrates the interdependence of God's people. The elderly often have the charism to bridge generation gaps before they are made: how many children have found understanding and love in the eyes and words and caresses of the aging! And how many old people have willingly subscribed to the inspired word that the 'crown of the aged is their childen's children' (*Prov* 17:6)!".[79]

[79] John Paul II, Address to the participants in the International Forum on Active Aging (5 September 1980), 5: *Insegnamenti di Giovanni Paolo II*, III, 2 (1980), 539.

1) *The transmission of life*

Cooperators in the love of God the Creator

28. With the creation of man and woman in his own image and likeness, God crowns and brings to perfection the work of his hands: he calls them to a special sharing in his love and in his power as Creator and Father, through their free and responsible cooperation in transmitting the gift of human life: "God blessed them, and God said to them, 'Be fruitful and multiply, and fill the earth and subdue it'".[80]

Thus the fundamental task of the family is to serve life, to actualize in history the original blessing of the Creator—that of transmitting by procreation the divine image from person to person.[81]

Fecundity is the fruit and the sign of conjugal love, the living testimony of the full reciprocal self-giving of the spouses: "While not making the other purposes of matrimony of less account, the true practice of conjugal love, and the whole meaning of the family life which results from it, have this aim: that the couple be ready with stout hearts to cooperate with the love of the

[80] *Gen* 1:28.
[81] Cf. *Gen* 5:1-3.

Creator and the Saviour, who through them will enlarge and enrich his own family day by day".[82]

However, the fruitfulness of conjugal love is not restricted solely to the procreation of children, even understood in its specifically human dimension: it is enlarged and enriched by all those fruits of moral, spiritual and supernatural life which the father and mother are called to hand on to their children, and through the children to the Church and to the world.

The Church's teaching and norm, always old yet always new

29. Precisely because the love of husband and wife is a unique participation in the mystery of life and of the love of God himself, the Church knows that she has received the special mission of guarding and protecting the lofty dignity of marriage and the most serious responsibility of the transmission of human life.

Thus, in continuity with the living tradition of the ecclesial community throughout history, the recent Second Vatican Council and the magisterium of my predecessor Paul VI, expressed above all in the Encyclical *Humanae Vitae*, have handed on to our times a truly prophetic proclamation, which reaffirms and reproposes with clarity the Church's teaching and norm,

[82] Second Vatican Ecumenical Council, Pastoral Constitution on the Church in the Modern World *Gaudium et Spes,* 50.

always old yet always new, regarding marriage and regarding the transmission of human life.

For this reason the Synod Fathers made the following declaration at their last assembly: "This Sacred Synod, gathered together with the Successor of Peter in the unity of faith, firmly holds what has been set forth in the Second Vatican Council (cf. *Gaudium et Spes,* 50) and afterwards in the Encyclical *Humanae Vitae,* particularly that love between husband and wife must be fully human, exclusive and open to new life (*Humanae Vitae,* 11; cf. 9, 12)".[83]

The Church stands for life

30. The teaching of the Church in our day is placed in a social and cultural context which renders it more difficult to understand and yet more urgent and irreplaceable for promoting the true good of men and women.

Scientific and technical progress, which contemporary man is continually expanding in his dominion over nature, not only offers the hope of creating a new and better humanity, but also causes ever greater anxiety regarding the future.

[83] *Propositio* 21. Section 11 of the Encyclical *Humanae Vitae* ends with the statement: "The Church, calling people back to the observance of the norms of the natural law, as interpreted by her constant doctrine, teaches that each and every marriage act must remain open to the transmission of life (*ut quilibet matrimonii usus ad vitam humanam procreandam per se destinatus permaneat*)": *AAS* 60 (1968), 488.

Some ask themselves if it is a good thing to be alive or if it would be better never to have been born; they doubt therefore if it is right to bring others into life when perhaps they will curse their existence in a cruel world with unforeseeable terrors. Others consider themselves to be the only ones for whom the advantages of technology are intended and they exclude others by imposing on them contraceptives or even worse means. Still others, imprisoned in a consumer mentality and whose sole concern is to bring about a continual growth of material goods, finish by ceasing to understand, and thus by refusing, the spiritual riches of a new human life. The ultimate reason for these mentalities is the absence in people's hearts of God, whose love alone is stronger than all the world's fears and can conquer them.

Thus an anti-life mentality is born, as can be seen in many current issues: one thinks, for example of a certain panic deriving from the studies of ecologists and futurologists on population growth, which sometimes exaggerate the danger of demographic increase to the quality of life.

But the Church firmly believes that human life, even if weak and suffering, is always a splendid gift of God's goodness. Against the pessimism and selfishness which cast a shadow over the world, the Church stands for life: in each human life she sees the splendour of that "Yes", that "Amen", who is Christ himself.[84] To the "No" which assails and afflicts the world, she replies with this living "Yes", thus defending the human person and the world from all who plot against and harm life.

The Church is called upon to manifest anew to everyone, with clear and stronger conviction, her will to promote human life by every means and to defend it against all attacks, in whatever condition or state of development it is found.

Thus the Church condemns as a grave offence against human dignity and justice all those activities of governments or other public authorities which attempt to limit in any way the freedom of couples in deciding about children. Consequently any violence applied by such authorities in favour of contraception or, still worse, of sterilization and procured abortion, must be altogether condemned and forcefully rejected. Likewise to be denounced as gravely unjust are cases where, in international relations, economic help given for the advancement of peoples is made conditional on programmes of contraception, sterilization and procured abortion.[85]

[84] Cf. 2 *Cor* 1:19; *Rev* 3:14.
[85] Cf. the Sixth Synod of Bishops' Message to Christian Families in the Modern World (24 October 1980), 5.

31.   The Church is certainly aware of the
many complex problems which couples in many
countries face today in their task of transmitting
life in a responsible way.   She also recognizes
the serious problem of population growth in the
form it has taken in many parts of the world and
its moral implications.

However, she holds that consideration in
depth of all the aspects of these problems offers
a new and stronger confirmation of the importance of the authentic teaching on birth regulation
reproposed in the Second Vatican Council and
in the Encyclical *Humanae Vitae.*

For this reason, together with the Synod
Fathers I feel it is my duty to extend a pressing
invitation to theologians, asking them to unite
their efforts in order to collaborate with the
hierarchical Magisterium and to commit themselves to the task of illustrating ever more clearly
the biblical foundations, the ethical grounds and
the personalistic reasons behind this doctrine.
Thus it will be possible, in the context of an
organic exposition, to render the teaching of the
Church on this fundamental question truly accessible to all people of good will, fostering a daily
more enlightened and profound understanding of
it: in this way God's plan will be ever more
completely fulfilled for the salvation of humanity
and for the glory of the Creator.

A united effort by theologians in this regard, inspired by a convinced adherence to the Magisterium, which is the one authentic guide for the People of God, is particularly urgent for reasons that include the close link between Catholic teaching on this matter and the view of the human person that the Church proposes: doubt or error in the field of marriage or the family involves obscuring to a serious extent the integral truth about the human person, in a cultural situation that is already so often confused and contradictory. In fulfilment of their specific role, theologians are called upon to provide enlightenment and a deeper understanding, and their contribution is of incomparable value and represents a unique and highly meritorious service to the family and humanity.

**In an integral vision
of the human person
and of his or her vocation**

32.   In the context of a culture which seriously distorts or entirely misinterprets the true meaning of human sexuality, because it separates it from its essential reference to the person, the Church more urgently feels how irreplaceable is her mission of presenting sexuality as a value and task of the whole person, created male and female in the image of God.

In this perspective the Second Vatican Council clearly affirmed that "when there is a question of harmonizing conjugal love with the responsible transmission of life, the moral aspect of any procedure does not depend solely on sincere intentions or on an evaluation of motives. It must be determined by *objective standards*. These, *based on the nature of the human person and his or her acts,* preserve the full sense of mutual self-giving and human procreation in the context of true love. Such a goal cannot be achieved unless the virtue of conjugal chastity is sincerely practised".[86]

It is precisely by moving from "an integral vision of man and of his vocation, not only his natural and earthly, but also his supernatural and eternal vocation",[87] that Paul VI affirmed that the teaching of the Church "is founded upon the inseparable connection, willed by God and unable to be broken by man on his own initiative, between the two meanings of the conjugal act: the unitive meaning and the procreative meaning".[88] And he concluded by re-emphasizing that there must be excluded as intrinsically immoral "every action which, either in anticipation of the conjugal act, or in its accomplishment, or in the development of its natural consequences, proposes, whether as an end or as a means, to render procreation impossible".[89]

[86] Pastoral Constitution on the Church in the Modern World *Gaudium et Spes,* 51.
[87] Encyclical *Humanae Vitae,* 7: *AAS* 60 (1968), 485.
[88] *Ibid.,* 12: *loc. cit.,* 488-489.
[89] *Ibid.,* 14: *loc. cit.,* 490.

When couples, by means of recourse to contraception, separate these two meanings that God the Creator has inscribed in the being of man and woman and in the dynamism of their sexual communion, they act as "arbiters" of the divine plan and they "manipulate" and degrade human sexuality—and with it themselves and their married partner—by altering its value of "total" self-giving. Thus the innate language that expresses the total reciprocal self-giving of husband and wife is overlaid, through contraception, by an objectively contradictory language, namely, that of not giving oneself totally to the other. This leads not only to a positive refusal to be open to life but also to a falsification of the inner truth of conjugal love, which is called upon to give itself in personal totality.

When, instead, by means of recourse to periods of infertility, the couple respect the inseparable connection between the unitive and procreative meanings of human sexuality, they are acting as "ministers" of God's plan and they "benefit from" their sexuality according to the original dynamism of "total" self-giving, without manipulation or alteration.[90]

In the light of the experience of many couples and of the data provided by the different human sciences, theological reflection is able to perceive and is called to study further *the difference, both anthropological and moral,* between contracep-

[90] *Ibid.,* 13: *loc. cit.,* 489.

tion and recourse to the rhythm of the cycle: it is a difference which is much wider and deeper than is usually thought, one which involves in the final analysis two irreconcilable concepts of the human person and of human sexuality. The choice of the natural rhythms involves accepting the cycle of the person, that is the woman, and thereby accepting dialogue, reciprocal respect, shared responsibility and self-control. To accept the cycle and to enter into dialogue means to recognize both the spiritual and corporal character of conjugal communion, and to live personal love with its requirement of fidelity. In this context the couple comes to experience how conjugal communion is enriched with those values of tenderness and affection which constitute the inner soul of human sexuality, in its physical dimension also. In this way sexuality is respected and promoted in its truly and fully human dimension, and is never "used" as an "object" that, by breaking the personal unity of soul and body, strikes at God's creation itself at the level of the deepest interaction of nature and person.

The Church as Teacher and Mother for couples in difficulty

33.   In the field of conjugal morality the Church is Teacher and Mother and acts as such.

As Teacher, she never tires of proclaiming the moral norm that must guide the responsible transmission of life. The Church is in no way the author or the arbiter of this norm. In obedience to the truth which is Christ, whose image is reflected in the nature and dignity of the human person, the Church interprets the moral norm and proposes it to all people of good will, without concealing its demands of radicalness and perfection.

As Mother, the Church is close to the many married couples who find themselves in difficulty over this important point of the moral life: she knows well their situation, which is often very arduous and at times truly tormented by difficulties of every kind, not only individual difficulties but social ones as well; she knows that many couples encounter difficulties not only in the concrete fulfilment of the moral norm but even in understanding its inherent values.

But it is one and the same Church that is both Teacher and Mother. And so the Church never ceases to exhort and encourage all to resolve whatever conjugal difficulties may arise without ever falsifying or compromising the truth: she is convinced that there can be no true contradiction between the divine law on transmitting life and that on fostering authentic married love.[91] Accordingly, the concrete pedagogy of the Church must always remain linked with her doctrine and never be separated from it. With the same con-

[91] Cf. Second Vatican Ecumenical Council, Pastoral Constitution on the Church in the Modern World *Gaudium et Spes*, 51.

viction as my predecessor, I therefore repeat:
"To diminish in no way the saving teaching of
Christ constitutes an eminent form of charity
for souls".[92]

On the other hand, authentic ecclesial pedagogy displays its realism and wisdom only by
making a tenacious and courageous effort to
create and uphold all the human conditions
—psychological, moral and spiritual—indispensable for understanding and living the moral value
and norm.

There is no doubt that these conditions must
include persistence and patience, humility and
strength of mind, filial trust in God and in his
grace, and frequent recourse to prayer and to the
sacraments of the Eucharist and of Reconciliation.[93] Thus strengthened, Christian husbands and
wives will be able to keep alive their awareness
of the unique influence that the grace of the sacrament of marriage has on every aspect of married
life, including therefore their sexuality: the gift of
the Spirit, accepted and responded to by husband
and wife, helps them to live their human sexuality
in accordance with God's plan and as a sign of
the unitive and fruitful love of Christ for his
Church.

But the necessary conditions also include
knowledge of the bodily aspect and the body's
rhythms of fertility. Accordingly, every effort

[92] Encyclical *Humanae Vitae*, 29: *AAS* 60 (1968), 501.
[93] Cf. *ibid.*, 25: *loc. cit.* 498-499.

must be made to render such knowledge accessible to all married people and also to young adults before marriage, through clear, timely and serious instruction and education given by married couples, doctors and experts. Knowledge must then lead to education in self-control: hence the absolute necessity for the virtue of chastity and for permanent education in it. In the Christian view, chastity by no means signifies rejection of human sexuality or lack of esteem for it: rather it signifies spiritual energy capable of defending love from the perils of selfishness and aggressiveness, and able to advance it towards its full realization.

With deeply wise and loving intuition, Paul VI was only voicing the experience of many married couples when he wrote in his Encyclical: "To dominate instinct by means of one's reason and free will undoubtedly requires ascetical practices, so that the affective manifestations of conjugal life may observe the correct order, in particular with regard to the observance of periodic continence. Yet this discipline which is proper to the purity of married couples, far from harming conjugal love, rather confers on it a higher human value. It demands continual effort, yet, thanks to its beneficent influence, husband and wife fully develop their personalities, being enriched with spiritual values. Such discipline bestows upon family life fruits of serenity and peace, and facilitates the solution of other problems; it

65

favours attention for one's partner, helps both parties to drive out selfishness, the enemy of true love, and deepens their sense of responsibility. By its means, parents acquire the capacity of having a deeper and more efficacious influence in the education of their offspring ".[94]

The moral progress of married people

34.   It is always very important to have a right notion of the moral order, its values and its norms; and the importance is all the greater when the difficulties in the way or respecting them become more numerous and serious.

Since the moral order reveals and sets forth the plan of God the Creator, for this very reason it cannot be something that harms man, something impersonal. On the contrary, by responding to the deepest demands of the human being created by God, it places itself at the service of that person's full humanity with the delicate and binding love whereby God himself inspires, sustains and guides every creature towards its happiness.

But man, who has been called to live God's wise and loving design in a responsible manner, is an historical being who day by day builds himself up through his many free decisions; and so he knows, loves and accomplishes moral good by stages of growth.

[94] *Ibid.*, 21: *loc. cit.*, 496.

Married people too are called upon to progress unceasingly in their moral life, with the support of a sincere and active desire to gain ever better knowledge of the values enshrined in and fostered by the law of God. They must also be supported by an upright and generous willingness to embody these values in their concrete decisions. They cannot however look on the law as merely an ideal to be achieved in the future: they must consider it as a command of Christ the Lord to overcome difficulties with constancy. "And so what is known as 'the law of gradualness' or step-by-step advance cannot be identified with 'gradualness of the law', as if there were different degrees or forms of precept in God's law for different individuals and situations. In God's plan, all husbands and wives are called in marriage to holiness, and this lofty vocation is fulfilled to the extent that the human person is able to respond to God's command with serene confidence in God's grace and in his or her own will".[95] On the same lines, it is part of the Church's pedagogy that husbands and wives should first of all recognize clearly the teaching of *Humanae Vitae* as indicating the norm for the exercise of their sexuality, and that they should endeavour to establish the conditions necessary for observing that norm.

As the Synod noted, this pedagogy embraces the whole of married life. Accordingly, the function of transmitting life must be integrated into

[95] John Paul II, Homily at the close of the Sixth Synod of Bishops (25 October 1980), 8: *AAS* 72 (1980), 1083.

the overall mission of Christian life as a whole, which without the Cross cannot reach the Resurrection. In such a context it is understandable that sacrifice cannot be removed from family life, but must in fact be wholeheartedly accepted if the love between husband and wife is to be deepened and become a source of intimate joy.

This shared progress demands reflection, instruction and suitable education on the part of the priests, religious and lay people engaged in family pastoral work: they will all be able to assist married people in their human and spiritual progress, a progress that demands awareness of sin, a sincere commitment to observe the moral law, and the ministry of reconciliation. It must also be kept in mind that conjugal intimacy involves the wills of two persons, who are however called to harmonize their mentality and behaviour: this requires much patience, understanding and time. Uniquely important in this field is unity of moral and pastoral judgment by priests, a unity that must be carefully sought and ensured, in order that the faithful may not have to suffer anxiety of conscience.[96]

It will be easier for married people to make progress if, with respect for the Church's teaching and with trust in the grace of Christ, and with the help and support of the pastors of souls and the entire ecclesial community, they are able to

[96] Cf. Paul VI, Encyclical *Humanae Vitae,* 28: *AAS* 60 (1968), 501.

discover and experience the liberating and inspiring value of the authentic love that is offered by the Gospel and set before us by the Lord's commandment.

Instilling conviction and offering practical help

35. With regard to the question of lawful birth regulation, the ecclesial community at the present time must take on the task of instilling conviction and offering practical help to those who wish to live out their parenthood in a truly responsible way.

In this matter, while the Church notes with satisfaction the results achieved by scientific research aimed at a more precise knowledge of the rhythms of women's fertility, and while it encourages a more decisive and wide-ranging extension of that research, it cannot fail to call with renewed vigour on the responsibility of all—doctors, experts, marriage counsellors, teachers and married couples—who can actually help married people to live their love with respect for the structure and finalities of the conjugal act which expresses that love. This implies a broader, more decisive and more systematic effort to make the natural methods of regulating fertility known, respected and applied.[97]

[97] Cf. John Paul II, Address to the Delegates of the Centre de Liaison des Equipes de Recherche (3 November 1979), 9: *Insegnamenti di Giovanni Paolo II*, II, 2 (1979), 1035; and

A very valuable witness can and should be given by those husbands and wives who through the joint exercise of periodic continence have reached a more mature personal responsibility with regard to love and life. As Paul VI wrote: "To them the Lord entrusts the task of making visible to people the holiness and sweetness of the law which unites the mutual love of husband and wife with their cooperation with the love of God the author of human life".[98]

2) *Education*

**The right and duty
of parents regarding education**

36. The task of giving education is rooted in the primary vocation of married couples to participate in God's creative activity: by begetting in love and for love a new person who has within himself or herself the vocation to growth and development, parents by that very fact take on the task of helping that person effectively to live a fully human life. As the Second Vatican Council recalled, "since parents have conferred life on their children, they have a most solemn obligation to educate their offspring. Hence, parents must be acknowledged as the first and foremost educators of their children. Their role as educators is so decisive that scarcely anything can compensate for

cf. Address to the participants in the First Congress for the Family of Africa and Europe (15 January 1981): *L'Osservatore Romano*, 16 January 1981.
   [98] Encyclical *Humanae Vitae*, 25: *AAS* 60 (1968), 499.

their failure in it. For it devolves on parents to create a family atmosphere so animated with love and reverence for God and others that a well-rounded personal and social development will be fostered among the children. Hence, the family is the first school of those social virtues which every society needs".[99]

The right and duty of parents to give education is *essential*, since it is connected with the transmission of human life; it is *original and primary* with regard to the educational role of others, on account of the uniqueness of the loving relationship between parents and children; and it is *irreplaceable and inalienable*, and therefore incapable of being entirely delegated to others or usurped by others.

In addition to these characteristics, it cannot be forgotten that the most basic element, so basic that it qualifies the educational role of parents, is *parental love*, which finds fulfilment in the task of education as it completes and perfects its service of life: as well as being a *source*, the parents' love is also the *animating principle* and therefore the *norm* inspiring and guiding all concrete educational activity, enriching it with the values of kindness, constancy, goodness, service, disinterestedness and self-sacrifice that are the most precious fruit of love.

[99] Declaration on Christian Education *Gravissimum Educationis*, 3.

37.   Even amid the difficulties of the work of
education, difficulties which are often greater today, parents must trustingly and courageously
train their children in the essential values of
human life. Children must grow up with a correct attitude of freedom with regard to material
goods, by adopting a simple and austere life style
and being fully convinced that "man is more
precious for what he is than for what he has".[100]

In a society shaken and split by tensions and
conflicts caused by the violent clash of various
kinds of individualism and selfishness, children
must be enriched not only with a sense of true
justice, which alone leads to respect for the personal dignity of each individual, but also and more
powerfully by a sense of true love, understood as
sincere solicitude and disinterested service with
regard to others, especially the poorest and those
in most need. The family is the first and fundamental school of social living: as a community of
love, it finds in self-giving the law that guides it
and makes it grow. The self-giving that inspires
the love of husband and wife for each other is
the model and norm for the self-giving that must
be practised in the relationships between brothers
and sisters and the different generations living
together in the family. And the communion and

[100] Second Vatican Ecumenical Council, Pastoral Constitution on the Church in the Modern World *Gaudium et Spes*, 35.

sharing that are part of everyday life in the home at times of joy and at times of difficulty are the most concrete and effective pedagogy for the active, responsible and fruitful inclusion of the children in the wider horizon of society.

Education in love as self-giving is also the indispensable premise for parents called to give their children a clear and delicate *sex education.* Faced with a culture that largely reduces human sexuality to the level of something commonplace, since it interprets and lives it in a reductive and impoverished way by linking it solely with the body and with selfish pleasure, the educational service of parents must aim firmly at a training in the area of sex that is truly and fully personal: for sexuality is an enrichment of the whole person—body, emotions and soul—and it manifests its inmost meaning in leading the person to the gift of self in love.

Sex education, which is a basic right and duty of parents, must always be carried out under their attentive guidance, whether at home or in educational centres chosen and controlled by them. In this regard, the Church reaffirms the law of subsidiarity, which the school is bound to observe when it cooperates in sex education, by entering into the same spirit that animates the parents.

In this context *education for chastity* is absolutely essential, for it is a virtue that develops a person's authentic maturity and makes him or her capable of respecting and fostering the "nuptial meaning" of the body. Indeed Christian parents, discerning the signs of God's call, will devote special attention and care to education in virginity or celibacy as the supreme form of that self-giving that constitutes the very meaning of human sexuality.

In view of the close links between the sexual dimension of the person and his or her ethical values, education must bring the children to a knowledge of and respect for the moral norms as the necessary and highly valuable guarantee for responsible personal growth in human sexuality.

For this reason the Church is firmly opposed to an often widespread form of imparting sex information dissociated from moral principles. That would merely be an introduction to the experience of pleasure and a stimulus leading to the loss of serenity—while still in the years of innocence—by opening the way to vice.

The mission to educate and the sacrament of marriage

38.   For Christian parents the mission to educate, a mission rooted, as we have said, in their participation in God's creating activity, has a new specific source in the sacrament of marriage, which consecrates them for the strictly Christian education of their children: that is to say, it calls upon them to share in the very authority and love of God the Father and Christ the Shepherd, and in the motherly love of the Church, and it enriches them with wisdom, counsel, fortitude and all the other gifts of the Holy Spirit in order to help

the children in their growth as human beings and as Christians.

The sacrament of marriage gives to the educational role the dignity and vocation of being really and truly a "ministry" of the Church at the service of the building up of her members. So great and splendid is the educational ministry of Christian parents that Saint Thomas has no hesitation in comparing it with the ministry of priests: "Some only propagate and guard spiritual life by a spiritual ministry: this is the role of the sacrament of Orders; others do this for both corporal and spiritual life, and this is brought about by the sacrament of marriage, by which a man and a woman join in order to beget offspring and bring them up to worship God".[101]

A vivid and attentive awareness of the mission that they have received with the sacrament of marriage will help Christian parents to place themselves at the service of their children's education with great serenity and trustfulness, and also with a sense of responsibility before God, who calls them and gives them the mission of building up the Church in their children. Thus in the case of baptized people, the family, called together by word and sacrament as the Church of the home, is both teacher and mother, the same as the worldwide Church.

---

[101] Saint Thomas Aquinas, *Summa contra Gentiles,* IV, 58.

39.   The mission to educate demands that Christian parents should present to their children all the topics that are necessary for the gradual maturing of their personality from a Christian and ecclesial point of view. They will therefore follow the educational lines mentioned above, taking care to show their children the depths of significance to which the faith and love of Jesus Christ can lead.   Furthermore, their awareness that the Lord is entrusting to them the growth of a child of God, a brother or sister of Christ, a temple of the Holy Spirit, a member of the Church, will support Christian parents in their task of strengthening the gift of divine grace in their children's souls.

The Second Vatican Council describes the content of Christian education as follows: " Such an education does not merely strive to foster maturity ... in the human person.   Rather, its principal aims are these: that as baptized persons are gradually introduced into a knowledge of the mystery of salvation, they may daily grow more conscious of the gift of faith which they have received; that they may learn to adore God the Father in spirit and in truth (cf. *Jn* 4: 23), especially through liturgical worship; that they may be trained to conduct their personal life in true righteousness and holiness, according to their new nature (*Eph* 4: 22-24), and thus grow to maturity, to the stature of the fullness of Christ (cf. *Eph*

4:13), and devote themselves to the upbuilding of the Mystical Body. Moreover, aware of their calling, they should grow accustomed to giving witness to the hope that is in them (cf. *1 Pt* 3:15), and to promoting the Christian transformation of the world".[102]

The Synod too, taking up and developing the indications of the Council, presented the educational mission of the Christian family as a true ministry through which the Gospel is transmitted and radiated, so that family life itself becomes an itinerary of faith and in some way a Christian initiation and a school of following Christ. Within a family that is aware of this gift, as Paul VI wrote, "all the members evangelize and are evangelized".[103]

By virtue of their ministry of educating, parents are, through the witness of their lives, the first heralds of the Gospel for their children. Furthermore, by praying with their children, by reading the word of God with them and by introducing them deeply through Christian initiation into the Body of Christ—both the Eucharistic and the ecclesial Body—they become fully parents, in that they are begetters not only of bodily life but also of the life that through the Spirit's renewal flows from the Cross and Resurrection of Christ.

---

[102] Declaration on Christian Education *Gravissimum Educationis,* 2.
[103] Apostolic Exhortation *Evangelii Nuntiandi,* 71: *AAS* 68 (1976), 60-61.

In order that Christian parents may worthily carry out their ministry of educating, the Synod Fathers expressed the hope that a suitable *catechism for families* would be prepared, one that would be clear, brief and easily assimilated by all. The Episcopal Conferences were warmly invited to contribute to producing this catechism.

Relations with other educating agents

40.   The family is the primary but not the only and exclusive educating community. Man's community aspect itself—both civil and ecclesial—demands and leads to a broader and more articulated activity resulting from well-ordered collaboration between the various agents of education. All these agents are necessary, even though each can and should play its part in accordance with the special competence and contribution proper to itself.[104]

The educational role of the Christian family therefore has a very important place in organic pastoral work. This involves a new form of cooperation between parents and Christian communities, and between the various educational groups and pastors. In this sense, the renewal of the Catholic school must give special attention

[104] Cf. Second Vatican Ecumenical Council, Declaration on Christian Education *Gravissimum Educationis,* 3.

both to the parents of the pupils and to the formation of a perfect educating community.

The right of parents to choose an education in conformity with their religious faith must be absolutely guaranteed.

The State and the Church have the obligation to give families all possible aid to enable them to perform their educational role properly. Therefore both the Church and the State must create and foster the institutions and activities that families justly demand, and the aid must be in proportion to the families' needs. However, those in society who are in charge of schools must never forget that the parents have been appointed by God himself as the first and principal educators of their children and that their right is completely inalienable.

But corresponding to their right, parents have a serious duty to commit themselves totally to a cordial and active relationship with the teachers and the school authorities.

If ideologies opposed to the Christian faith are taught in the schools, the family must join with other families, if possible through family associations, and with all its strength and with wisdom help the young not to depart from the faith. In this case the family needs special assistance from pastors of souls, who must never forget that parents have the inviolable right to entrust their children to the ecclesial community.

41.   Fruitful married love expresses itself in serving life in many ways. Of these ways, begetting and educating children are the most immediate, specific and irreplaceable.   In fact, every act of true love towards a human being bears witness to and perfects the spiritual fecundity of the family, since it is an act of obedience to the deep inner dynamism of love as self-giving to others.

For everyone this perspective is full of value and commitment, and it can be an inspiration in particular for couples who experience physical sterility.

Christian families, recognizing with faith all human beings as children of the same heavenly Father, will respond generously to the children of other families, giving them support and love not as outsiders but as members of the one family of God's children. Christian parents will thus be able to spread their love beyond the bonds of flesh and blood, nourishing the links that are rooted in the spirit and that develop through concrete service to the children of other families, who are often without even the barest necessities.

Christian families will be able to show greater readiness to adopt and foster children who have lost their parents or have been abandoned by them. Rediscovering the warmth of affection of a family, these children will be able to experience God's loving and provident fatherhood witnessed to by Christian parents, and they will thus be able to grow up with serenity and confidence in life. At the same time the whole family will be enriched with the spiritual values of a wider fraternity.

Family fecundity must have an unceasing "creativity", a marvellous fruit of the Spirit of God, who opens the eyes of the heart to discover the new needs and sufferings of our society and gives courage for accepting them and responding to them. A vast field of activity lies open to families: today, even more preoccupying than child abandonment is the phenomenon of social and cultural exclusion, which seriously affects the elderly, the sick, the disabled, drug addicts, ex-prisoners, etc.

This broadens enormously the horizons of the parenthood of Christian families: these and many other urgent needs of our time are a challenge to their spiritually fruitful love. With families and through them, the Lord Jesus continues to "have compassion" on the multitudes.

III – PARTICIPATING IN THE DEVELOPMENT OF SOCIETY

The family as the first and vital cell of society

42.   "Since the Creator of all things has established the conjugal partnership as the beginning and basis of human society", the family is "the first and vital cell of society".[105]

---

[105] Second Vatican Ecumenical Council, Decree on the Apostolate of the Laity *Apostolicam Actuositatem*, 11.

The family has vital and organic links with society, since it is its foundation and nourishes it continually through its role of service to life: it is from the family that citizens come to birth and it is within the family that they find the first school of the social virtues that are the animating principle of the existence and development of society itself.

Thus, far from being closed in on itself, the family is by nature and vocation open to other families and to society, and undertakes its social role.

Family life as an experience of communion and sharing

43.　　The very experience of communion and sharing that should characterize the family's daily life represents its first and fundamental contribution to society.

The relationships between the members of the family community are inspired and guided by the law of "free giving". By respecting and fostering personal dignity in each and every one as the only basis for value, this free giving takes the form of heartfelt acceptance, encounter and dialogue, disinterested availability, generous service and deep solidarity.

Thus the fostering of authentic and mature communion between persons within the family is the first and irreplaceable school of social life, an example and stimulus for the broader community relationships marked by respect, justice, dialogue and love.

The family is thus, as the Synod Fathers recalled, the place of origin and the most effective means for humanizing and personalizing society: it makes an original contribution in depth to building up the world, by making possible a life that is properly speaking human, in particular by guarding and transmitting virtues and "values". As the Second Vatican Council states, in the family "the various generations come together and help one another to grow wiser and to harmonize personal rights with the other requirements of social living".[106]

Consequently, faced with a society that is running the risk of becoming more and more depersonalized and standardized and therefore inhuman and dehumanizing, with the negative results of many forms of escapism—such as alcoholism, drugs and even terrorism—the family possesses and continues still to release formidable energies capable of taking man out of his anonymity, keeping him conscious of his personal dignity, enriching him with deep humanity and actively placing him, in his uniqueness and unrepeatability, within the fabric of society.

[106] Pastoral Constitution on the Church in the Modern World *Gaudium et Spes*, 52.

44.   The social role of the family certainly
cannot stop short at procreation and education,
even if this constitutes its primary and irreplaceable form of expression.

Families therefore, cither singly or in asso-
ciation, can and should devote themselves to manifold social service activities, especially in favour
of the poor, or at any rate for the benefit of
all people and situations that cannot be reached
by the public authorities' welfare organization.

The social contribution of the family has an
original character of its own, one that should be
given greater recognition and more decisive encouragement, especially as the children grow up,
and actually involving all its members as much
as possible.[107]

In particular, note must be taken of the
ever greater importance in our society of hospitality in all its forms, from opening the
door of one's home and still more of one's heart
to the pleas of one's brothers and sisters, to
concrete efforts to ensure that every family has
its own home, as the natural environment that
preserves it and makes it grow. In a special way
the Christian family is called upon to listen to the
Apostle's recommendation: "Practise hospitality",[108] and therefore, imitating Christ's example

---

[107] Cf. Second Vatican Ecumenical Council, Decree on the
Apostolate of the Laity *Apostolicam Actuositatem*, 11.
 [108] *Rom* 12:13.

and sharing in his love, to welcome the brother or sister in need: "Whoever gives to one of these little ones even a cup of cold water because he is a disciple, truly, I say to you, he shall not lose his reward".[109]

The social role of families is called upon to find expression also in the form of *political intervention*: families should be the first to take steps to see that the laws and institutions of the State not only do not offend but support and positively defend the rights and duties of the family. Along these lines, families should grow in awareness of being "protagonists" of what is known as "family politics" and assume responsibility for transforming society; otherwise families will be the first victims of the evils that they have done no more than note with indifference. The Second Vatican Council's appeal to go beyond an individualistic ethic therefore also holds good for the family as such.[110]

Society at the service of the family

45.   Just as the intimate connection between the family and society demands that the family be open to and participate in society and its development, so also it requires that society should never

---

[109] *Mt* 10:42.
[110] Cf. Pastoral Constitution on the Church in the Modern World *Gaudium et Spes*, 30.

fail in its fundamental task of respecting and fostering the family.

The family and society have complementary functions in defending and fostering the good of each and every human being. But society—more specifically the State—must recognize that "the family is a society in its own original right" [111] and so society is under a grave obligation in its relations with the family to adhere to the principle of subsidiarity.

By virtue of this principle, the State cannot and must not take away from families the functions that they can just as well perform on their own or in free associations; instead it must positively favour and encourage as far as possible responsible initiative by families. In the conviction that the good of the family is an indispensable and essential value of the civil community, the public authorities must do everything possible to ensure that familes have all those aids—economic, social, educational, political and cultural assistance—that they need in order to face all their responsibilities in a human way.

The charter of family rights

46.   The ideal of mutual support and development between the family and society is often very seriously in conflict with the reality of their separation and even opposition.

[111] Second Vatican Ecumenical Council, Declaration on Religious Freedom *Dignitatis Humanae*, 5.

In fact, as was repeatedly denounced by the Synod, the situation experienced by many families in various countries is highly problematical, if not entirely negative: institutions and laws unjustly ignore the inviolable rights of the family and of the human person; and society, far from putting itself at the service of the family, attacks it violently in its values and fundamental requirements. Thus the family, which in God's plan is the basic cell of society and a subject of rights and duties before the State or any other community, finds itself the victim of society, of the delays and slowness with which it acts, and even of its blatant injustice.

For this reason, the Church openly and strongly defends the rights of the family against the intolerable usurpations of society and the State. In particular, the Synod Fathers mentioned the following rights of the family:

— the right to exist and progress as a family, that is to say, the right of every human being, even if he or she is poor, to found a family and to have adequate means to support it;

— the right to exercise its responsibility regarding the transmission of life and to educate children;

— the right to the intimacy of conjugal and family life;

— the right to the stability of the bond and of the institution of marriage;

— the right to believe in and profess one's faith and to propagate it;

— the right to bring up children in accordance with the family's own traditions and religious and cultural values, with the necessary instruments, means and institutions;

— the right, especially of the poor and the sick, to obtain physical, social, political and economic security;

— the right to housing suitable for living family life in a proper way;

— the right to expression and to representation, either directly or through associations, before the economic, social and cultural public authorities and lower authorities;

— the right to form associations with other families and institutions, in order to fulfil the family's role suitably and expeditiously;

— the right to protect minors by adequate institutions and legislation from harmful drugs, pornography, alcoholism, etc.;

— the right to wholesome recreation of a kind that also fosters family values;

— the right of the elderly to a worthy life and a worthy death;

— the right to emigrate as a family in search of a better life.[112]

Acceding to the Synod's explicit request, the Holy See will give prompt attention to studying these suggestions in depth and to the preparation

[112] Cf. *Propositio* 42.

of a Charter of Rights of the Family, to be
presented to the quarters and authorities concerned.

The Christian family's grace and responsibility

47.   The social role that belongs to every family pertains by a new and original right to the
Christian family, which is based on the sacrament
of marriage. By taking up the human reality of
the love between husband and wife in all its
implications, the sacrament gives to Christian
couples and parents a power and a commitment
to live their vocation as lay people and therefore
to "seek the kingdom of God by engaging in
temporal affairs and by ordering them according
to the plan of God".[113]

The social and political role is included in
the kingly mission of service in which Christian
couples share by virtue of the sacrament of marriage, and they receive both a command which
they cannot ignore and a grace which sustains
and stimulates them.

The Christian family is thus called upon to
offer everyone a witness of generous and disinterested dedication to social matters, through a
"preferential option" for the poor and disadvan-
taged. Therefore, advancing in its following of
the Lord by special love for all the poor, it must

---

[113] Second Vatican Ecumenical Council, Dogmatic Constitution on the Church *Lumen Gentium*, 31.

have special concern for the hungry, the poor, the old, the sick, drug victims and those who have no family.

48.   In view of the worldwide dimension of various social questions nowadays, the family has seen its role with regard to the development of society extended in a completely new way: it now also involves cooperating for a new international order, since it is only in worldwide solidarity that the enormous and dramatic issues of world justice, the freedom of peoples and the peace of humanity can be dealt with and solved.

The spiritual communion between Christian families, rooted in a common faith and hope and given life by love, constitutes an inner energy that generates, spreads and develops justice, reconciliation, fraternity and peace among human beings. In so far as it is a "small-scale Church", the Christian family is called upon, like the "large-scale Church", to be a sign of unity for the world and in this way to exercise its prophetic role by bearing witness to the Kingdom and peace of Christ, towards which the whole world is journeying.

Christian families can do this through their educational activity—that is to say by presenting to their children a model of life based on the values of truth, freedom, justice and love—both through active and responsible involvement

in the authentically human growth of society and
its institutions, and by supporting in various
ways the associations specifically devoted to international issues.

IV – SHARING IN THE LIFE
AND MISSION OF THE CHURCH

**The family,
within the mystery of the Church**

49.   Among the fundamental tasks of the
Christian family is its ecclesial task: the family
is placed at the service of the building up of the
Kingdom of God in history by participating in
the life and mission of the Church.

In order to understand better the foundations,
the contents and the characteristics of this participation, we must examine the many profound
bonds linking the Church and the Christian
family and establishing the family as a "Church
in miniature" (*Ecclesia domestica*),[114] in such a
way that in its own way the family is a living
image and historical representation of the mystery of the Church.

It is, above all, the Church as Mother that
gives birth to, educates and builds up the
Christian family, by putting into effect in its
regard the saving mission which she has received

---

[114] Cf. Second Vatican Ecumenical Council, Dogmatic Con-
stitution on the Church *Lumen Gentium,* 11; Decree on the
Apostolate of the Laity *Apostolicam Actuositatem,* 11; Pope
John Paul II, Homily for the opening of the Sixth Synod of
Bishops (26 September 1980), 3: *AAS* 72 (1980), 1008.

from her Lord. By proclaiming the word of God, the Church reveals to the Christian family its true identity, what it is and should be according to the Lord's plan; by celebrating the sacraments, the Church enriches and strengthens the Christian family with the grace of Christ for its sanctification to the glory of the Father; by the continuous proclamation of the new commandment of love, the Church encourages and guides the Christian family to the service of love, so that it may imitate and relive the same self-giving and sacrificial love that the Lord Jesus has for the entire human race.

In turn, the Christian family is grafted into the mystery of the Church to such a degree as to become a sharer, in its own way, in the saving mission proper to the Church: by virtue of the sacrament, Christian married couples and parents "in their state and way of life have their own special gift among the People of God".[115] For this reason they not only *receive* the love of Christ and become a *saved* community, but they are also called upon to *communicate* Christ's love to their brethren, thus becoming a *saving* community. In this way, while the Christian family is a fruit and sign of the supernatural fecundity of the Church, it stands also as a symbol, witness and participant of the Church's motherhood.[116]

[115] Second Vatican Ecumenical Council, Dogmatic Constitution on the Church *Lumen Gentium,* 11.
[116] Cf. *ibid.,* 41.

50.   The Christian family is called upon to
take part actively and responsibly in the mission
of the Church in a way that is original and specific,
by placing itself, in what it is and what it does as
an "intimate community of life and love", at the
service of the Church and of society.

Since the Christian family is a community in
which the relationships are renewed by Christ
through faith and the sacraments, the family's
sharing in the Church's mission should follow
a community pattern: the spouses together *as
a couple,* the parents and children *as a family,*
must live their service to the Church and to the
world. They must be "of one heart and soul" [117]
in faith, through the shared apostolic zeal that
animates them, and through their shared commitment to works of service in the ecclesial and
civil communities.

The Christian family also builds up the Kingdom of God in history through the everyday
realities that concern and distinguish its *state of
life.* It is thus in *the love between husband and
wife and between the members of the family*—a
love lived out in all its extraordinary richness of
values and demands: totality, oneness, fidelity and
fruitfulness [118]—that the Christian family's participation in the prophetic, priestly and kingly

[117] *Acts* 4:32.
[118] Cf. Paul VI, Encyclical *Humanae Vitae,* 9: *AAS* 60
(1968), 486-487.

93

mission of Jesus Christ and of his Church finds expression and realization. Therefore, love and life constitute the nucleus of the saving mission of the Christian family in the Church and for the Church.

The Second Vatican Council recalls this fact when it writes: "Families will share their spiritual riches generously with other families too. Thus the Christian family, which springs from marriage as a reflection of the loving covenant uniting Christ with the Church, and as a participation in that covenant will manifest to all people the Saviour's living presence in the world, and the genuine nature of the Church. This the family will do by the mutual love of the spouses, by their generous fruitfulness, their solidarity and faithfulness, and by the loving way in which all the members of the family work together".[119]

Having laid the *foundation* of the participation of the Christian family in the Church's mission, it is now time to illustrate its *substance in reference to Jesus Christ as Prophet, Priest and King*—three aspects of a single reality—by presenting the Christian family as 1) a believing and evangelizing community, 2) a community in dialogue with God, and 3) a community at the service of man.

[119] Pastoral Constitution on the Church in the Modern World *Gaudium et Spes,* 48.

1) *The Christian family as a believing and evangelizing community*

**Faith as the discovery
and admiring awareness
of God's plan for the family**

51.   As a sharer in the life and mission of the Church, which listens to the word of God with reverence and proclaims it confidently,[120] *the Christian family fulfils its prophetic role by welcoming and announcing the word of God*: it thus becomes more and more each day a believing and evangelizing community.

Christian spouses and parents are required to offer "the obedience of faith".[121]   They are called upon to welcome the word of the Lord which reveals to them the marvellous news—the Good News—of their conjugal and family life sanctified and made a source of sanctity by Christ himself.   Only in faith can they discover and admire with joyful gratitude the dignity to which God has deigned to raise marriage and the family, making them a sign and meeting-place of the loving covenant between God and man, between Jesus Christ and his bride, the Church.

The very preparation for Chistian mariage is itself a journey of faith. It is a special opportunity for the engaged to rediscover and deepen the

---

[120] Cf. Second Vatican Council, Dogmatic Constitution on Divine Revelation *Dei Verbum,* 1.
[121] *Rom* 16:26.

faith received in Baptism and nourished by their Christian upbringing. In this way they come to recognize and freely accept their vocation to follow Christ and to serve the Kingdom of God in the married state.

The celebration of the sacrament of marriage is the basic moment of the faith of the couple. This sacrament, in essence, is the proclamation in the Church of the Good News concerning married love. It is the word of God that "reveals" and "fulfils" the wise and loving plan of God for the married couple, giving them a mysterious and real share in the very love with which God himself loves humanity. Since the sacramental celebration of marriage is itself a proclamation of the word of God, it must also be a "profession of faith" within and with the Church, as a community of believers, on the part of all those who in different ways participate in its celebration.

This profession of faith demands that it be prolonged in the life of the married couple and of the family. God, who called the couple *to* marriage, continues to call them *in* marriage.[122] In and through the events, problems, difficulties and circumstances of everyday life, God comes to them, revealing and presenting the concrete "demands" of their sharing in the love of Christ for his Church in the particular family, social

[122] Cf. Paul VI, Encyclical *Humanae Vitae*, 25: *AAS* 60 (1968), 498.

and ecclesial situation in which they find themselves.

The discovery of and obedience to the plan of God on the part of the conjugal and family community must take place in "togetherness", through the human experience of love between husband and wife, between parents and children, lived in the Spirit of Christ.

Thus the little domestic Church, like the greater Church, needs to be constantly and intensely evangelized: hence its duty regarding permanent education in the faith.

The Christian family's ministry of evangelization

52.   To the extent in which the Christian family accepts the Gospel and matures in faith, it becomes an evangelizing community. Let us listen again to Paul VI: "The family, like the Church, ought to be a place where the Gospel is transmitted and from which the Gospel radiates. In a family which is conscious of this mission, all the members evangelize and are evangelized. The parents not only communicate the Gospel to their children, but from their children they can themselves receive the same Gospel as deeply lived by them. And such a family becomes the evangelizer of many other families, and of the neighbourhood of which it forms part".[123]

As the Synod repeated, taking up the appeal

---

[123] Apostolic Exhortation *Evangelii Nuntiandi*, 71: *AAS* 68 (1976), 60-61.

which I launched at Puebla, the future of evangelization depends in great part on the Church of the home.[124] This apostolic mission of the family is rooted in Baptism and receives from the grace of the sacrament of marriage new strength to transmit the faith, to sanctify and transform our present society according to God's plan.

Particularly today, the Christian family has a special vocation to witness to the paschal covenant of Christ by constantly radiating the joy of love and the certainty of the hope for which it must give an account: "The Christian family loudly proclaims both the present virtues of the Kingdom of God and the hope of a blessed life to come".[125]

The absolute need for family catechesis emerges with particular force in certain situations that the Church unfortunately experiences in some places: "In places where anti-religious legislation endeavours even to prevent education in the faith, and in places where widespread unbelief or invasive secularism makes real religious growth practically impossible, 'the Church of the home' remains the one place where children and young people can receive an authentic catechesis".[126]

---

[124] Cf. Address to the Third General Assembly of the Bishops of Latin American (28 January 1979), IV a: *AAS* 71 (1979), 204.
[125] Second Vatican Ecumenical Council, Dogmatic Constitution on the Church *Lumen Gentium,* 35.
[126] John Paul II, Apostolic Exhortation *Catechesi Tradendae,* 68: *AAS* 71 (1979), 1334.

53.   The ministry of evangelization carried out by Christian parents is original and irreplaceable. It assumes the characteristics typical of family life itself, which should be interwoven with love, simplicity, practicality and daily witness.[127]

The family must educate the children for life in such a way that each one may fully perform his or her role according to the vocation received from God. Indeed, the family that is open to transcendent values, that serves its brothers and sisters with joy, that fulfils its duties with generous fidelity, and is aware of its daily sharing in the mystery of the glorious Cross of Christ, becomes the primary and most excellent seedbed of vocations to a life of consecration to the Kingdom of God.

The parents' ministry of evangelization and catechesis ought to play a part in their children's lives also during adolescence and youth, when the children, as often happens, challenge or even reject the Christian faith received in earlier years. Just as in the Church the work of evangelization can never be separated from the sufferings of the apostle, so in the Christian family parents must face with courage and great interior serenity the difficulties that their ministry of evangelization sometimes encounters in their own children.

It should not be forgotten that the service

---

[127] Cf. *ibid.*, 36: *loc. cit.* 1308.

rendered by Christian spouses and parents to the Gospel is essentially an ecclesial service. It has its place within the context of the whole Church as an evangelized and evangelizing community. In so far as the ministry of evangelization and catechesis of the Church of the home is rooted in and derives from the one mission of the Church and is ordained to the upbuilding of the one Body of Christ,[128] it must remain in intimate communion and collaborate responsibly with all the other evangelizing and catechetical activities present and at work in the ecclesial community at the diocesan and parochial levels.

**To preach the Gospel
to the whole creation**

54.   Evangelization, urged on within by irrepressible missionary zeal, is characterized by a universality without boundaries. It is the response to Christ's explicit and unequivocal command: "Go into all the world and preach the Gospel to the whole creation ".[129]

The Christian family's faith and evangelizing mission also possesses this catholic missionary inspiration. The sacrament of marriage takes up and reproposes the task of defending and spreading the faith, a task that has its roots in Baptism and Confirmation,[130] and makes Christian married

[128] Cf. *1 Cor* 12:4-6; *Eph* 4:12-13.
[129] *Mk* 16:15.
[130] Cf. Second Vatican Ecumenical Council, Dogmatic Constitution on the Church *Lumen Gentium*, 11.

couples and parents witnesses of Christ "to the end of the earth",[131] missionaries, in the true and proper sense, of love and life.

A form of missionary activity can be exercised even within the family. This happens when some member of the family does not have the faith or does not practise it with consistency. In such a case the other members must give him or her a living witness of their own faith in order to encourage and support him or her along the path towards full acceptance of Christ the Saviour.[132]

Animated in its own inner life by missionary zeal, the Church of the home is also called to be a luminous sign of the presence of Christ and of his love for those who are "far away", for families who do not yet believe, and for those Christian families who no longer live in accordance with the faith that they once received. The Christian family is called to enlighten "by its example and its witness... those who seek the truth".[133]

Just as at the dawn of Christianity Aquila and Priscilla were presented as a missionary couple,[134] so today the Church shows forth her perennial newness and fruitfulness by the presence of Christian couples and families who dedicate at

[131] *Acts* 1:8.
[132] Cf. *1 Pt* 3:1-2.
[133] Second Vatican Ecumenical Council, Dogmatic Constitution on the Church *Lumen Gentium*, 35; cf. Decree on the Apostolate of the Laity *Apostolicam Actuositatem*, 11.
[134] Cf. *Acts* 18; *Rom* 16:3-4.

least a part of their lives to working in missionary
territories, proclaiming the Gospel and doing service to their fellowman in the love of Jesus Christ.

Christian families offer a special contribution
to the missionary cause of the Church by fostering
missionary vocations among their sons and daughters [135] and, more generally, "by training their
children from childhood to recognize God's love
for all people ".[136]

2) *The Christian family*
as a community in dialogue with God

**The Church's sanctuary
in the home**

55.   The proclamation of the Gospel and its
acceptance in faith reach their fullness in the
celebration of the sacraments. The Church which
is a believing and evangelizing community is also
a priestly people invested with the dignity and
sharing in the power of Christ the High Priest
of the New and Eternal Covenant.[137]

The Christian family too is part of this priestly
people which is the Church. By means of the
sacrament of marriage, in which it is rooted and
from which it draws its nourishment, the Christian family is continuously vivified by the Lord

[135] Cf. Second Vatican Ecumenical Council, Decree on the
Church's Missionary Activity *Ad Gentes,* 39.

[136] Second Vatican Ecumenical Council, Decree on the
Apostolate of the Laity *Apostolicam Actuositatem,* 30.

[137] Cf. Second Vatican Ecumenical Council, Dogmatic Constitution on the Church *Lumen Gentium,* 10.

Jesus and called and engaged by him in a dialogue with God through the sacraments, through the offering of one's life, and through prayer.

This is the *priestly role* which the Christian family can and ought to exercise in intimate communion with the whole Church, through the daily realities of married and family life. In this way the Christian family *is called to be sanctified and to sanctify the ecclesial community and the world.*

Marriage as a sacrament of mutual sanctification and an act of worship

56.   The sacrament of marriage is the specific source and original means of sanctification for Christian married couples and families. It takes up again and makes specific the sanctifying grace of Baptism. By virtue of the mystery of the death and Resurrection of Christ, of which the spouses are made part in a new way by marriage, conjugal love is purified and made holy: "This love the Lord has judged worthy of special gifts, healing, perfecting and exalting gifts of grace and of charity".[138]

The gift of Jesus Christ is not exhausted in the actual celebration of the sacrament of marriage, but rather accompanies the married couple throughout their lives. This fact is explicitly recalled by the Second Vatican Council when it

---

[138] Second Vatican Ecumenical Council, Pastoral Constitution on the Church in the Modern World *Gaudium et Spes,* 49.

says that Jesus Christ "abides with them so that, just as he loved the Church and handed himself over on her behalf, the spouses may love each other with perpetual fidelity through mutual self-bestowal... For this reason, Christian spouses have a special sacrament by which they are fortified and receive a kind of consecration in the duties and dignity of their state. By virtue of this sacrament, as spouses fulfil their conjugal and family obligations, they are penetrated with the Spirit of Christ, who fills their whole lives with faith, hope and charity. Thus they increasingly advance towards their own perfection, as well as towards their mutual sanctification, and hence contribute jointly to the glory of God".[139]

Christian spouses and parents are included in the universal call to sanctity. For them this call is specified by the sacrament they have celebrated and is carried out concretely in the realities proper to their conjugal and family life.[140] This gives rise to the grace and requirement of an authentic and profound *conjugal and family spirituality* that draws its inspiration from the themes of creation, covenant, cross, resurrection, and sign, which were stressed more than once by the Synod.

Christian marriage, like the other sacraments, "whose purpose is to sanctify people, to build up the body of Christ, and finally, to give wor-

<hr>

[139] *Ibid.*, 48.
[140] Cf. Second Vatican Ecumenical Council, Dogmatic Constitution on the Church *Lumen Gentium*, 41.

ship to God",[141] is in itself a liturgical action glorifying God in Jesus Christ and in the Church. By celebrating it, Christian spouses profess their gratitude to God for the sublime gift bestowed on them of being able to live in their married and family lives the very love of God for people and that of the Lord Jesus for the Church, his bride.

Just as husbands and wives receive from the sacrament the gift and responsibility of translating into daily living the sanctification bestowed on them, so the same sacrament confers on them the grace and moral obligation of transforming their whole lives into a "spiritual sacrifice".[142] What the Council says of the laity applies also to Christian spouses and parents, especially with regard to the earthly and temporal realities that characterize their lives: "As worshippers leading holy lives in every place, the laity consecrate the world itself to God".[143]

Marriage and the Eucharist

57. The Christian family's sanctifying role is grounded in Baptism and has its highest expression in the Eucharist, to which Christian marriage is intimately connected. The Second Vatican Council drew attention to the unique relation-

[141] Second Vatican Ecumenical Council, Constitution on the Sacred Liturgy *Sacrosanctum Concilium,* 59.
[142] Cf. *1 Pt* 2:5; Second Vatican Ecumenical Council, Dogmatic Constitution on the Church *Lumen Gentium,* 34.
[143] Second Vatican Ecumenical Council, Dogmatic Constitution on the Church *Lumen Gentium,* 34.

ship between the Eucharist and marriage by requesting that "marriage normally be celebrated within the Mass".[144] To understand better and live more intensely the graces and responsibilities of Christian marriage and family life, it it altogether necessary to rediscover and strengthen this relationship.

The Eucharist is the very source of Christian marriage. The Eucharistic Sacrifice, in fact, represents Christ's covenant of love with the Church, sealed with his blood on the Cross.[145] In this sacrifice of the New and Eternal Covenant, Christian spouses encounter the source from which their own marriage covenant flows, is interiorly structured and continuously renewed. As a representation of Christ's sacrifice of love for the Church, the Eucharist is a fountain of charity. In the Eucharistic gift of charity the Christian family finds the foundation and soul of its "communion" and its "mission": by partaking in the Eucharistic bread, the different members of the Christian family become one body, which reveals and shares in the wider unity of the Church. Their sharing in the Body of Christ that is "given up" and in his Blood that is "shed" becomes a never-ending source of missionary and apostolic dynamism for the Christian family.

[144] Constitution on the Sacred Liturgy *Sacrosanctum Concilium*, 78.
[145] Cf. *Jn* 19:34.

58. An essential and permanent part of the Christian family's sanctifying role consists in accepting the call to conversion that the Gospel addresses to all Christians, who do not always remain faithful to the "newness" of the Baptism that constitutes them "saints". The Christian family too is sometimes unfaithful to the law of baptismal grace and holiness proclaimed anew in the sacrament of marriage.

Repentance and mutual pardon within the bosom of the Christian family, so much a part of daily life, receive their specific sacramental expression in Christian Penance. In the Encyclical *Humanae Vitae,* Paul VI wrote of married couples: "And if sin should still keep its hold over them, let them not be discouraged, but rather have recourse with humble perseverance to the mercy of God, which is abundantly poured forth in the sacrament of Penance".[146]

The celebration of this sacrament acquires special significance for family life. While they discover in faith that sin contradicts not only the covenant with God, but also the covenant between husband and wife and the communion of the family, the married couple and the other members of the family are led to an encounter with God, who is "rich in mercy",[147] who bestows on them his

---

[146] Section 25: *AAS* 60 (1968), 499.
[147] *Eph* 2:4.

love which is more powerful than sin,[148] and who reconstructs and brings to perfection the marriage covenant and the family communion.

Family prayer

59. The Church prays for the Christian family and educates the family to live in generous accord with the priestly gift and role received from Christ the High Priest. In effect, the baptismal priesthood of the faithful, exercised in the sacrament of marriage, constitutes the basis of a priestly vocation and mission for the spouses and family by which their daily lives are transformed into "spiritual sacrifices acceptable to God through Jesus Christ".[149] This transformation is achieved not only by celebrating the Eucharist and the other sacraments and through offering themselves to the glory of God, but also through a life of prayer, through prayerful dialogue with the Father, through Jesus Christ, in the Holy Spirit.

Family prayer has its own characteristic qualities. It is prayer offered *in common,* husband and wife together, parents and children together. Communion in prayer is both a consequence of and a requirement for the communion bestowed by the sacraments of Baptism and Matrimony. The words with which the

---

[148] Cf. John Paul II, Encyclical *Dives in Misericordia,* 13: *AAS* 72 (1980), 1218-1219.

[149] *1 Pt* 2:5.

Lord Jesus promises his presence can be applied to the members of the Christian family in a special way: "Again I say to you, if two of you agree on earth about anything they ask it will be done for them by my Father in heaven. For where two or three are gathered in my name, there am I in the midst of them".[150]

Family prayer has for its very own object *family life itself,* which in all its varying circumstances is seen as a call from God and lived as a filial response to his call. Joys and sorrows, hopes and disappointments, births and birthday celebrations, wedding anniversaries of the parents, departures, separations and home-comings, important and far-reaching decisions, the death of those who are dear, etc.—all of these mark God's loving intervention in the family's history. They should be seen as suitable moments for thanksgiving, for petition, for trusting abandonment of the family into the hands of their common Father in heaven. The dignity and responsibility of the Christian family as the domestic Church can be achieved only with God's unceasing aid, which will surely be granted if it is humbly and trustingly petitioned in prayer.

Educators in prayer

60. By reason of their dignity and mission, Christian parents have the specific responsibility of educating their children in prayer, introducing

[150] *Mt* 18:19-20.

them to gradual discovery of the mystery of God and to personal dialogue with him: "It is particularly in the Christian family, enriched by the grace and the office of the sacrament of Matrimony, that from the earliest years children should be taught, according to the faith received in Baptism, to have a knowledge of God, to worship him and to love their neighbour".[151]

The concrete example and living witness of parents is fundamental and irreplaceable in educating their children to pray. Only by praying together with their children can a father and mother—exercising their royal priesthood—penetrate the innermost depths of their children's hearts and leave an impression that the future events in their lives will not be able to efface. Let us again listen to the appeal made by Paul VI to parents: "Mothers, do you teach your children the Christian prayers? Do you prepare them, in conjunction with the priests, for the sacraments that they receive when they are young: Confession, Communion and Confirmation? Do you encourage them when they are sick to think of Christ suffering, to invoke the aid of the Blessed Virgin and the saints? Do you say the family Rosary together? And you, fathers, do you pray with your children, with the whole domestic

[151] Second Vatican Ecumenical Council, Declaration on Christian Education *Gravissimum Educationis*, 3; cf. Pope John Paul II, Apostolic Exhortation *Catechesi Tradendae*, 36: *AAS* 71 (1979), 1308.

community, at least sometimes? Your example of honesty in thought and action, joined to some common prayer, is a lesson for life, an act of worship of singular value. In this way you bring peace to your homes: *Pax huic domui.* Remember, it is thus that you build up the Church".[152]

Liturgical prayer and private prayer

61. There exists a deep and vital bond between the prayer of the Church and the prayer of the individual faithful, as has been clearly reaffirmed by the Second Vatican Council.[153] An important purpose of the prayer of the domestic Church is to serve as the natural introduction for the children to the liturgical prayer of the whole Church, both in the sense of preparing for it and of extending it into personal, family and social life. Hence the need for gradual participation by all the members of the Christian family in the celebration of the Eucharist, especially on Sundays and feast days, and of the other sacraments, particularly the sacraments of Christian initiation of the children. The directives of the Council opened up a new possibility for the Christian family when it listed the family among those

---

[152] General Audience Address, 11 August 1976: *Insegnamenti di Paolo VI,* XIV (1976), 640.
[153] Cf. Constitution on the Sacred Liturgy *Sacrosanctum Concilium,* 12.

111

groups to whom it recommends the recitation of the Divine Office in common.[154] Likewise, the Christian family will strive to celebrate at home, and in a way suited to the members, the times and feasts of the liturgical year.

As preparation for the worship celebrated in church, and as its prolongation in the home, the Christian family makes use of private prayer, which presents a great variety of forms. While this variety testifies to the extraordinary richness with which the Spirit vivifies Christian prayer, it serves also to meet the various needs and life situations of those who turn to the Lord in prayer. Apart from morning and evening prayers, certain forms of prayer are to be expressly encouraged, following the indications of the Synod Fathers, such as reading and meditating on the word of God, preparation for the reception of the sacraments, devotion and consecration to the Sacred Heart of Jesus, the various forms of veneration of the Blessed Virgin Mary, grace before and after meals, and observance of popular devotions.

While respecting the freedom of the children of God, the Church has always proposed certain practices of piety to the faithful with particular solicitude and insistence. Among these should be mentioned the recitation of the Rosary: "We now desire, as a continuation of the thought of

---

[154] Cf. *Institutio Generalis de Liturgia Horarum,* 27.

our predecessors, to recommend strongly the recitation of the family Rosary ... There is no doubt that ... the Rosary should be considered as one of the best and most efficacious prayers in common that the Christian family is invited to recite. We like to think, and sincerely hope, that when the family gathering becomes a time of prayer the Rosary is a frequent and favoured manner of praying".[155] In this way authentic devotion to Mary, which finds expression in sincere love and generous imitation of the Blessed Virgin's interior spiritual attitude, constitutes a special instrument for nourishing loving communion in the family and for developing conjugal and family spirituality. For she who is the Mother of Christ and of the Church is in a special way the Mother of Christian families, of domestic Churches.

Prayer and life

62.   It should never be forgotten that prayer constitutes an essential part of Christian life, understood in its fullness and centrality. Indeed, prayer is an important part of our very humanity: it is "the first expression of man's inner truth, the first condition for authentic freedom of spirit".[156]

Far from being a form of escapism from

[155] Paul VI, Apostolic Exhortation *Marialis Cultus*, 52, 54: *AAS* 66 (1974), 160-161.
[156] John Paul II, Address at the Mentorella Shrine (29 October 1978): *Insegnamenti di Giovanni Paolo II*, I (1978), 78-79.

everyday commitments, prayer constitutes the strongest incentive for the Christian family to assume and comply fully with all its responsibilities as the primary and fundamental cell of human society. Thus the Christian family's actual participation in the Church's life and mission is in direct proportion to the fidelity and intensity of the prayer with which it is united with the fruitful vine that is Christ the Lord.[157]

The fruitfulness of the Christian family in its specific service to human advancement, which of itself cannot but lead to the transformation of the world, derives from its living union with Christ, nourished by the Liturgy, by self-oblation and by prayer.[158]

3) *The Christian family*
    as a community at the service of man

The new commandment of love

63.　The Church, a prophetic, priestly and kingly people, is endowed with the mission of bringing all human beings to accept the word of God in faith, to celebrate and profess it in the sacraments and in prayer, and to give expression to it in the concrete realities of life in accordance with the gift and new commandment of love.

---

[157] Cf. Second Vatican Ecumenical Council, Decree on the Apostolate of the Laity *Apostolicam Actuositatem,* 4.
[158] Cf. John Paul I, Address to the Bishops of the Twelfth Pastoral Region of the United States of America (21 September 1978): *AAS* 70 (1978), 767.

The law of Christian life is to be found not in a written code, but in the personal action of the Holy Spirit who inspires and guides the Christian. It is the "law of the Spirit of life in Christ Jesus": [159] "God's love has been poured into our hearts through the Holy Spirit who has been given to us".[160]

This is true also for the Christian couple and family. Their guide and rule of life is the Spirit of Jesus poured into their hearts in the celebration of the sacrament of Matrimony. In continuity with Baptism in water and the Spirit, marriage sets forth anew the evangelical law of love, and with the gift of the Spirit engraves it more profoundly on the hearts of Christian husbands and wives. Their love, purified and saved, is a fruit of the Spirit acting in the hearts of believers and constituting, at the same time, the fundamental commandment of their moral life to be lived in responsible freedom.

Thus the Christian family is inspired and guided by the new law of the Spirit and, in intimate communion with the Church, the kingly people, it is called to exercise its "service" of love towards God and towards its fellow human beings. Just as Christ exercises his royal power by serving us,[161] so also the Christian finds the authentic meaning of his participation in the kingship of his Lord in sharing his spirit and

[159] *Rom* 8:2.
[160] *Rom* 5:5.
[161] Cf. *Mk* 10:45.

practice of service to man. "Christ has communicated this power to his disciples that they might be established in royal freedom and that by self-denial and a holy life they might conquer the reign of sin in themselves (cf. *Rom* 6:12). Further, he has shared this power so that by serving him in their fellow human beings they might through humility and patience lead their brothers and sisters to that King whom to serve is to reign. For the Lord wishes to spread his kingdom by means of the laity also, a kingdom of truth and life, a kingdom of holiness and grace, a kingdom of justice, love and peace. In this kingdom, creation itself will be delivered out of its slavery to corruption and into the freedom of the glory of the children of God (cf. *Rom* 8:21)".[162]

To discover the image of God in each brother and sister

64.   Inspired and sustained by the new commandment of love, the Christian family welcomes, respects and serves every human being, considering each one in his or her dignity as a person and as a child of God.

It should be so especially between husband and wife and within the family, through a daily effort to promote a truly personal community, initiated and fostered by an inner communion of

[162] Second Vatican Ecumenical Council, Dogmatic Constitution on the Church *Lumen Gentium,* 36.

love. This way of life should then be extended to the wider circle of the ecclesial community of which the Christian family is a part. Thanks to love within the family, the Church can and ought to take on a more homelike or family dimension, developing a more human and fraternal style of relationships.

Love, too, goes beyond our brothers and sisters of the same faith since "everybody is my brother or sister". In each individual, especially in the poor, the weak, and those who suffer or are unjustly treated, love knows how to discover the face of Christ, and discover a fellow human being to be loved and served.

In order that the family may serve man in a truly evangelical way, the instructions of the Second Vatican Council must be carefully put into practice: "That the exercise of such charity may rise above any deficiencies in fact and even in appearance, certain fundamentals must be observed. Thus, attention is to be paid to the image of God in which our neighbour has been created, and also to Christ the Lord to whom is really offered whatever is given to a needy person". [163]

While building up the Church in love, the Christian family places itself at the service of the human person and the world, really bringing about the "human advancement" whose substance

---

[163] Decree of the Apostolate of the Laity *Apostolicam Actuositatem*, 8.

was given in summary form in the Synod's Message to families: "Another task for the family is to form persons in love and also to practise love in all its relationships, so that it does not live closed in on itself, but remains open to the community, moved by a sense of justice and concern for others, as well as by a consciousness of its responsibility towards the whole of society".[164]

[164] Cf. the Sixth Synod of Bishops' Message to Christian Families in the Modern World (24 October 1980), 12.

PASTORAL CARE OF THE FAMILY: STAGES, STRUCTURES, AGENTS AND SITUATIONS

I – STAGES OF PASTORAL CARE OF THE FAMILY

**The Church accompanies
the Christian family
on its journey through life**

65. Like every other living reality, the family too is called upon to develop and grow. After the preparation of engagement and the sacramental celebration of marriage, the couple begin their daily journey towards the progressive actuation of the values and duties of marriage itself.

In the light of faith and by virtue of hope, the Christian family too shares, in communion with the Church, in the experience of the earthly pilgrimage towards the full revelation and manifestation of the Kingdom of God.

Therefore, it must be emphasized once more that the pastoral intervention of the Church in support of the family is a matter of urgency. Every effort should be made to strengthen and develop pastoral care for the family, which should be treated as a real matter of priority, in the certainty that future evangelization depends largely on the domestic Church.[165]

The Church's pastoral concern will not be limited only to the Christian families closest at hand; it will extend its horizons in harmony with the Heart of Christ, and will show itself to be even more lively for families in general and for those families in particular which are in difficult or irregular situations. For all of them the Church will have a word of truth, goodness, understanding, hope and deep sympathy with their sometimes tragic difficulties. To all of them she will offer her disinterested help so that they can come closer to that model of a family which the Creator intended from "the beginning" and which Christ has renewed with his redeeming grace.

The Church's pastoral action must be progressive, also in the sense that it must follow the family, accompanying it step by step in the different stages of its formation and development.

Preparation for marriage

66.   More than ever necessary in our times is preparation of young people for marriage and family life. In some countries it is still the families themselves that, according to ancient cus-

---

[165] Cf. John Paul II, Address to the Third General Assembly of the Bishops of Latin America (28 January 1979), IV a: *AAS* 71 (1979), 204.

toms, ensure the passing on to young people of the values concerning married and family life, and they do this through a gradual process of education or initiation. But the changes that have taken place within almost all modern societies demand that not only the family but also society and the Church should be involved in the effort of properly preparing young people for their future responsibilities. Many negative phenomena which are today noted with regret in family life derive from the fact that, in the new situations, young people not only lose sight of the correct hierarchy of values but, since they no longer have certain criteria of behaviour, they do not know how to face and deal with the new difficulties. But experience teaches that young people who have been well prepared for family life generally succeed better than others.

This is even more applicable to Christian marriage, which influences the holiness of large numbers of men and women. The Church must therefore promote better and more intensive programmes of marriage preparation, in order to eliminate as far as possible the difficulties that many married couples find themselves in, and even more in order to favour positively the establishing and maturing of successful marriages.

Marriage preparation has to be seen and put into practice as a gradual and continuous process. It includes three main stages: remote, proximate and immediate preparation.

Remote preparation begins in early childhood,

in that wise family training which leads children to discover themselves as beings endowed with a rich and complex psychology and with a particular personality with its own strengths and weaknesses. It is the period when esteem for all authentic human values is instilled, both in interpersonal and in social relationships, with all that this signifies for the formation of character, for the control and right use of one's inclinations, for the manner of regarding and meeting people of the opposite sex, and so on. Also necessary, especially for Christians, is solid spiritual and catechetical formation that will show that marriage is a true vocation and mission, without excluding the possibility of the total gift of self to God in the vocation to the priestly or religious life.

Upon this basis there will subsequently and gradually be built up the *proximate preparation,* which—from the suitable age and with adequate catechesis, as in a catechumenal process—involves a more specific preparation for the sacraments, as it were a rediscovery of them. This renewed catechesis of young people and others preparing for Christian marriage is absolutely necessary in order that the sacrament may be celebrated and lived with the right moral and spiritual dispositions. The religious formation of young people should be integrated, at the right moment and in accordance with the various concrete requirements, with a preparation for life as a couple. This preparation will present marriage as an interpersonal relationship of a man and a woman that has to be continually developed, and it will encourage those concerned to study the nature of conjugal sexuality and responsible parenthood, with the essential medical and biological knowledge connected with it. It will also acquaint those concerned with correct methods for the education of children, and will assist them in gaining the basic requisites for well-ordered family life, such as stable work, sufficient financial resources, sensible administration, notions of housekeeping.

Finally, one must not overlook preparation for the family apostolate, for fraternal solidarity and collaboration with other families, for active membership in groups, associations, movements and undertakings set up for the human and Christian benefit of the family.

The *immediate preparation* for the celebration of the sacrament of Matrimony should take place in the months and weeks immediately preceding the wedding, so as to give a new meaning, content and form to the so-called premarital enquiry required by Canon Law. This preparation is not only necessary in every case, but is also more urgently needed for engaged couples that still manifest shortcomings or difficulties in Christian doctrine and practice.

Among the elements to be instilled in this journey of faith, which is similar to the catechumenate, there must also be a deeper knowledge of the mystery of Christ and the Church, of the meaning of grace and of the responsibility of

Christian marriage, as well as preparation for taking an active and conscious part in the rites of the marriage liturgy.

The Christian family and the whole of the ecclesial community should feel involved in the different phases of the preparation for marriage, which have been described only in their broad outlines. It is to be hoped that the Episcopal Conferences, just as they are concerned with appropriate initiatives to help engaged couples to be more aware of the seriousness of their choice and also to help pastors of souls to make sure of the couples' proper dispositions, so they will also take steps to see that there is issued a *Directory for the Pastoral Care of the Family.* In this they should lay down, in the first place, the minimum content, duration and method of the "Preparation Courses", balancing the different aspects—doctrinal, pedagogical, legal and medical—concerning marriage, and structuring them in such a way that those preparing for marriage will not only receive an intellectual training but will also feel a desire to enter actively into the ecclesial community.

Although one must not underestimate the necessity and obligation of the immediate preparation for marriage—which would happen if dispensations from it were easily given—nevertheless such preparation must always be set forth and put into practice in such a way that omitting it is not an impediment to the celebration of marriage.

67.   Christian marriage normally requires a liturgical celebration expressing in social and community form the essentially ecclesial and sacramental nature of the conjugal covenant between baptized persons.

Inasmuch as it is a *sacramental action of sanctification,* the celebration of marriage—inserted into the liturgy, which is the summit of the Church's action and the source of her sanctifying power [166]—must be *per se* valid, worthy and fruitful.   This opens a wide field for pastoral solicitude, in order that the needs deriving from the nature of the conjugal covenant, elevated into a sacrament, may be fully met, and also in order that the Church's discipline regarding free consent, impediments, the canonical form and the actual rite of the celebratiton may be faithfully observed.   The celebration should be simple and dignified, according to the norms of the competent authorities of the Church.   It is also for them—in accordance with concrete circumstances of time and place and in conformity with the norms issued by the Apostolic See [167]—to include in the liturgical celebration such elements proper to each culture which serve to express more clearly the profound human and religious significance of the marriage contract, provided that

---

[166] Cf. Second Vatican Ecumenical Council, Constitution on the Sacred Liturgy *Sacrosanctum Concilium,* 10.
[167] Cf. *Ordo Celebrandi Matrimonium,* 17.

such elements contain nothing that is not in harmony with Christian faith and morality.

Inasmuch as it is a *sign,* the liturgical celebration should be conducted in such a way as to constitute, also in its external reality, a proclamation of the word of God and a profession of faith on the part of the community of believers. Pastoral commitment will be expressed here through the intelligent and careful preparation of the Liturgy of the Word and through the education to faith of those participating in the celebration and in the first place the couple being married.

Inasmuch as it is a *sacramental action of the Church,* the liturgical celebration of marriage should involve the Christian community, with the full, active and responsible participation of all those present, according to the place and task of each individual: the bride and bridegroom, the priest, the witnesses, the relatives, the friends, the other members of the faithful, all of them members of an assembly that manifests and lives the mystery of Christ and his Church. For the celebration of Christian marriage in the sphere of ancestral cultures or traditions, the principles laid down above should be followed.

**Celebration of marriage
and evangelization
of non-believing baptized persons**

68.   Precisely because in the celebration of the
sacrament very special attention must be devoted
to the moral and spiritual dispositions of those
being married, in particular to their faith, we
must here deal with a not infrequent difficulty in
which the pastors of the Church can find themselves in the context of our secularized society.

In fact, the faith of the person asking the
Church for marriage can exist in different degrees,
and it is the primary duty of pastors to bring about
a rediscovery of this faith and to nourish it and
bring it to maturity. But pastors must also understand the reasons that lead the Church also to
admit to the celebration of marriage those who
are imperfectly disposed.

The sacrament of Matrimony has this specific
element that distinguishes it from all the other
sacraments: it is the sacrament of something that
was part of the very economy of creation; it is
the very conjugal covenant instituted by the
Creator "in the beginning". Therefore the decision of a man and a woman to marry in accordance with this divine plan, that is to say,
the decision to commit by their irrevocable conjugal consent their whole lives in indissoluble love
and unconditional fidelity, really involves, even
if not in a fully conscious way, an attitude of profound obedience to the will of God, an attitude
which cannot exist without God's grace. They

127

have thus already begun what is in a true and proper sense a journey towards salvation, a journey which the celebration of the sacrament and the immediate preparation for it can complement and bring to completion, given the uprightness of their intention.

On the other hand it is true that in some places engaged couples ask to be married in church for motives which are social rather than genuinely religious. This is not surprising. Marriage, in fact, is not an event that concerns only the persons actually getting married. By its very nature it is also a social matter, committing the couple being married in the eyes of society. And its celebration has always been an occasion of rejoicing that brings together families and friends. It therefore goes without saying that social as well as personal motives enter into the request to be married in church.

Nevertheless, it must not be forgotten that these engaged couples, by virtue of their Baptism, are already really sharers in Christ's marriage Covenant with the Church, and that, by their right intention, they have accepted God's plan regarding marriage and therefore at least implicitly consent to what the Church intends to do when she celebrates marriage. Thus, the fact that motives of a social nature also enter into the request is not enough to justify refusal on the part of pastors. Moreover, as the Second Vatican Council teaches, the sacraments by words and ritual elements nourish and strengthen faith: [168] that faith towards which the married couple are already journeying by reason of the uprightness of their intention, which Christ's grace certainly does not fail to favour and support.

As for wishing to lay down further criteria for admission to the ecclesial celebration of marriage, criteria that would concern the level of faith of those to be married, this would above all involve grave risks. In the first place, the risk of making unfounded and discriminatory judgments; secondly, the risk of causing doubts about the validity of marriages already celebrated, with grave harm to Christian communities, and new and unjustified anxieties to the consciences of married couples; one would also fall into the danger of calling into question the sacramental nature of many marriages of brethren separated from full communion with the Catholic Church, thus contradicting ecclesial tradition.

However, when in spite of all efforts engaged couples show that they reject explicitly and formally what the Church intends to do when the marriage of baptized persons is celebrated, the pastor of souls cannot admit them to the celebration of marriage. In spite of his reluctance to do so, he has the duty to take note of the situation and to make it clear to those concerned that, in these circumstances, it is not the Church

---

[168] Cf. Second Vatican Ecumenical Council, Constitution on the Sacred Liturgy *Sacrosanctum Concilium,* 59.

129

that is placing an obstacle in the way of the celebration that they are asking for, but themselves.

Once more there appears in all its urgency the need for evangelization and catechesis before and after marriage, effected by the whole Christian community, so that every man and woman that gets married celebrates the sacrament of Matrimony not only validly but also fruitfully.

Pastoral care after marriage

69.   The pastoral care of the regularly established family signifies, in practice, the commitment of all the members of the local ecclesial community to helping the couple to discover and live their new vocation and mission. In order that the family may be ever more a true community of love, it is necessary that all its members should be helped and trained in their responsibilities as they face the new problems that arise, in mutual service, and in active sharing in family life.

This holds true especially for young families, which, finding themselves in a context of new values and responsibilities, are more vulnerable, especially in the first years of marriage, to possible difficulties, such as those created by adaptation to life together or by the birth of children. Young married couples should learn to accept willingly, and make good use of, the discreet, tactful and generous help offered by other couples that already have more experience of married and family life. Thus, within the ecclesial community—the great family made up of Christian families—there will take place a mutual exchange of presence and help among all the families, each one putting at the service of the others its own experience of life, as well as the gifts of faith and grace. Animated by a true apostolic spirit, this assistance from family to family will constitute one of the simplest, most effective and most accessible means for transmitting from one to another those Christian values which are both the starting-point and goal of all pastoral care. Thus young families will not limit themselves merely to receiving, but in their turn, having been helped in this way, will become a source of enrichment for other longer established families, through their witness of life and practical contribution.

In her pastoral care of young families, the Church must also pay special attention to helping them to live married love responsibly in relationship with its demands of communion and service to life. She must likewise help them to harmonize the intimacy of home life with the generous shared work of building up the Church and society. When children are born and the married couple becomes a family in the full and specific sense, the Church will still remain close to the parents in order that they may accept their children and love them as a gift received from the Lord of life, and joyfully accept the task of serving them in their human and Christian growth.

Pastoral activity is always the dynamic expression of the reality of the Church, committed to her mission of salvation. Family pastoral care too—which is a particular and specific form of pastoral activity—has as its operative principle and responsible agent the Church herself, through her structures and workers.

The ecclesial community and in particular the parish

70.   The Church, which is at the same time a saved and a saving community, has to be considered here under two aspects: as universal and particular. The second aspect is expressed and actuated in the diocesan community, which is pastorally divided up into lesser communities, of which the parish is of special importance.

Communion with the universal Church does not hinder but rather guarantees and promotes the substance and originality of the various particular Churches. These latter remain the more immediate and more effective subjects of operation for putting the pastoral care of the family into practice. In this sense every local Church and, in more particular terms, every parochial community, must become more vividly aware of the grace and responsibility that it receives from the Lord in order that it may promote the pastoral care of the family. No plan for organized pastoral work, at any level, must ever fail to take into consideration the pastoral care of the family.

Also to be seen in the light of this responsibility is the importance of the proper preparation of all those who will be more specifically engaged in this kind of apostolate. Priests and men and women religious, from the time of their formation, should be oriented and trained progressively and thoroughly for the various tasks. Among the various initiatives I am pleased to emphasize the recent establishment in Rome, at the Pontifical Lateran University, of a Higher Institute for the study of the problems of the family. Institutes of this kind have also been set up in some dioceses. Bishops should see to it that as many priests as possible attend specialized courses there before taking on parish responsibilities. Elsewhere, formation courses are periodically held at Higher Institutes of theological and pastoral studies. Such initiatives should be encouraged, sustained, increased in number, and of course are also open to lay people who intend to use their professional skills (medical, legal, psychological, social or educational) to help the family.

The family

71.   But it is especially necessary to recognize the unique place that, in this field, belongs to the mission of married couples and Christian families, by virtue of the grace received in the sacrament. This mission must be placed at the service of the

building up of the Church, the establishing of
the Kingdom of God in history. This is demanded
as an act of docile obedience to Christ the Lord.
For it is he who, by virtue of the fact that marriage
of baptized persons has been raised to a sacrament,
confers upon Christian married couples a special
mission as apostles, sending them as workers into
his vineyard, and, in a very special way, into this
field of the family.

In this activity, married couples act in communion and collaboration with the other members of the Church, who also work for the family,
contributing their own gifts and ministries. This
apostolate will be exercised in the first place
within the families of those concerned, through
the witness of a life lived in conformity with
the divine law in all its aspects, through the
Christian formation of the children, through
helping them to mature in faith, through education to chastity, through preparation for life,
through vigilance in protecting them from the
ideological and moral dangers with which they
are often threatened, through their gradual and
responsible inclusion in the ecclesial community
and the civil community, through help and advice
in choosing a vocation, through mutual help
among family members for human and Christian
growth together, and so on. The apostolate of
the family will also become wider through works
of spiritual and material charity towards other
families, especially those most in need of help
and support, towards the poor, the sick, the old,

the handicapped, orphans, widows, spouses that
have been abandoned, unmarried mothers and
mothers-to-be in difficult situations who are
tempted to have recourse to abortion, and so on.

Associations of families
for families

72.   Still within the Church, which is the subject
responsible for the pastoral care of the family,
mention should be made of the various groupings
of members of the faithful in which the mystery
of Christ's Church is in some measure manifested
and lived.   One should therefore recognize and
make good use of—each one in relationship to
its own characteristics, purposes, effectiveness
and methods—the different ecclesial communities,
the various groups and the numerous movements
engaged in various ways, for different reasons and
at different levels, in the pastoral care of the
family.

For this reason the Synod expressly recognized
the useful contribution made by such associations
of spirituality, formation and apostolate. It will
be their task to foster among the faithful a lively
sense of solidarity, to favour a manner of living
inspired by the Gospel and by the faith of the
Church, to form consciences according to Christian values and not according to the standards
of public opinion; to stimulate people to perform works of charity for one another and for
others with a spirit of openness which will make

Christian families into a true source of light and a wholesome leaven for other families.

It is similarly desirable that, with a lively sense of the common good, Christian families should become actively engaged, at every level, in other non-ecclesial associations as well. Some of these associations work for the preservation, transmission and protection of the wholesome ethical and cultural values of each people, the development of the human person, the medical, juridical and social protection of mothers and young children, the just advancement of women and the struggle against all that is detrimental to their dignity, the increase of mutual solidarity, knowledge of the problems connected with the responsible regulation of fertility in accordance with natural methods that are in conformity with human dignity and the teaching of the Church. Other associations work for the building of a more just and human world; for the promotion of just laws favouring the right social order with full respect for the dignity and every legitimate freedom of the individual and the family, on both the national and the international level; for collaboration with the school and with the other institutions that complete the education of children, and so forth.

As well as the family, which is the object but above all the subject of pastoral care of the family, one must also mention the other main agents in this particular sector.

Bishops and priests

73.   The person principally responsible in the diocese for the pastoral care of the family is the Bishop. As father and pastor, he must exercise particular solicitude in this clearly priority sector of pastoral care. He must devote to it personal interest, care, time, personnel and resources, but above all personal support for the families and for all those who, in the various diocesan structures, assist him in the pastoral care of the family. It will be his particular care to make the diocese ever more truly a "diocesan family", a model and source of hope for the many families that belong to it. The setting up of the Pontifical Council for the Family is to be seen in this light: to be a sign of the importance that I attribute to pastoral care for the family in the world, and at the same time to be an effective instrument for aiding and promoting it at every level.

The Bishops avail themselves especially of the priests, whose task—as the Synod expressly emphasized—constitutes an essential part of the Church's ministry regarding marriage and the family. The same is true of deacons to whose care this sector of pastoral work may be entrusted.

Their responsibility extends not only to moral and liturgical matters but to personal and social matters as well. They must support the family in its difficulties and sufferings, caring for its members and helping them to see their lives in the light of the Gospel. It is not superfluous to note that from this mission, if it is exercised with due discernment and with a truly apostolic spirit, the minister of the Church draws fresh encouragement and spiritual energy for his own vocation too and for the exercise of his ministry.

Priests and deacons, when they have received timely and serious preparation for this apostolate, must unceasingly act towards families as fathers, brothers, pastors and teachers, assisting them with the means of grace and enlightening them with the light of truth. Their teaching and advice must therefore always be in full harmony with the authentic Magisterium of the Church, in such a way as to help the People of God to gain a correct sense of the faith, to be subsequently applied to practical life. Such fidelity to the Magisterium will also enable priests to make every effort to be united in their judgments, in order to avoid troubling the consciences of the faithful.

In the Church, the pastors and the laity share in the prophetic mission of Christ: the laity do so by witnessing to the faith by their words and by their Christian lives; the pastors do so by distinguishing in that witness what is the expression of genuine faith from what is less in harmony with the light of faith; the family, as a Christian community, does so through its special sharing and witness of faith. Thus there begins a dialogue also between pastors and families. Theologians and experts in family matters can be of great help in this dialogue, by explaining exactly the content of the Church's Magisterium and the content of the experience of family life. In this way the teaching of the Magisterium becomes better understood and the way is opened to its progressive development. But it is useful to recall that the proximate and obligatory norm in the teaching of the faith—also concerning family matters—belongs to the hierarchical Magisterium. Clearly defined relationships between theologians, experts in family matters and the Magisterium are of no little assistance for the correct understanding of the faith and for promoting—within the boundaries of the faith—legitimate pluralism.

Men and women religious

74. The contribution that can be made to the apostolate of the family by men and women religious and consecrated persons in general finds its primary, fundamental and original expression precisely in their consecration to God. By reason of this consecration, "for all Christ's faithful re-

ligious recall that wonderful marriage made by
God, which will be fully manifested in the future
age, and in which the Church has Christ for her
only spouse",[169] and they are witnesses to that
universal charity which, through chastity em-
braced for the Kingdom of heaven, makes them
ever more available to dedicate themselves
generously to the service of God and to the
works of the apostolate.

Hence the possibility for men and women
religious, and members of Secular Institutes
and other institutes of perfection, either individ-
ually or in groups, to develop their service to
families, with particular solicitude for children,
especially if they are abandoned, unwanted, or-
phaned, poor or handicapped. They can also visit
families and look after the sick; they can foster
relationships of respect, and charity towards
one-parent families or families that are in difficulties or are separated; they can offer their
own work of teaching and counselling in the
preparation of young people for marriage, and
in helping couples towards truly responsible parenthood; they can open their own houses for
simple and cordial hospitality, so that families can
find there the sense of God's presence and gain a
taste for prayer and recollection, and see the
practical examples of lives lived in charity and fraternal joy as members of the larger family of God.

[169] Second Vatican Ecumenical Council, Decree on Renewal
of Religious Life *Perfectae Caritatis*, 12.

I would like to add a most pressing exhortation to the heads of institutes of consecrated life to consider—always with substantial respect for the proper and original charism of each one—the apostolate of the family as one of the priority tasks, rendered even more urgent by the present state of the world.

Lay specialists

75.   Considerable help can be given to families by lay specialists (doctors, lawyers, psychologists, social workers, consultants, etc.) who either as individuals or as members of various associations and undertakings offer their contribution of enlightenment, advice, orientation and support.   To these people one can well apply the exhortations that I had the occasion to address to the Confederation of Family Advisory Bureaux of Christian Inspiration: "Yours is a commitment that well deserves the title of mission, so noble are the aims that it pursues, and so determining, for the good of society and the Christian community itself, are the results that derive from it ...   All that you succeed in doing to support the family is destined to have an effectiveness that goes beyond its own sphere and reaches other people too and has an effect on society.   The future of the world and of the Church passes through the family".[170]

[170] John Paul II, Address to the Confederation of Family Advisory Bureaux of Christian Inspiration (29 November 1980), 3-4: *Insegnamenti di Giovanni Paolo II*, III, 2 (1980), 1453-1454.

76. This very important category in modern
life deserves a word of its own. It is well known
that the means of social communication "affect,
and often profoundly, the minds of those who use
them, under the affective and intellectual aspect
and also under the moral and religious aspect",
especially in the case of young people.[171] They
can thus exercise a beneficial influence on the
life and habits of the family and on the education
of children, but at the same time they also conceal
"snares and dangers that cannot be ignored".[172]
They could also become a vehicle—sometimes
cleverly and systematically manipulated, as unfortunately happens in various countries of the
world—for divisive ideologies and distorted
ways of looking at life, the family, religion and
morality, attitudes that lack respect for man's true
dignity and destiny.

This danger is all the more real inasmuch as
"the modern life style—especially in the more
industrialized nations—all too often causes families to abandon their responsibility to educate
their children. Evasion of this duty is made easy
for them by the presence of television and certain
publications in the home, and in this way they

[171] Paul VI, Message for the Third Social Communications
Day (7 April 1969): *AAS* 61 (1969), 455.
[172] John Paul II, Message for the 1980 World Social Communications Day (1 May 1980): *Insegnamenti di Giovanni
Paolo II,* III, 1 (1980), 1042.

keep their children's time and energies occupied".[173] Hence "the duty... to protect the young from the forms of aggression they are subjected to by the mass media", and to ensure that the use of the media in the family is carefully regulated. Families should also take care to seek for their children other forms of entertainment that are more wholesome, useful and physically, morally and spiritually formative, "to develop and use to advantage the free time of the young and direct their energies".[174]

Furthermore, because the means of social communication, like the school and the environment, often have a notable influence on the formation of children, parents as recipients must actively ensure the moderate, critical, watchful and prudent use of the media, by discovering what effect they have on their children and by controlling the use of the media in such a way as to "train the conscience of their children to express calm and objective judgments, which will then guide them in the choice or rejection of programmes available".[175]

With equal commitment parents will endeavour to influence the selection and the preparation of the programmes themselves, by keeping in

[173] John Paul II, Message for the 1981 World Social Communications Day (10 May 1981), 5: *L'Osservatore Romano*, 22 May 1981.
[174] *Ibid.*
[175] Paul VI, Message for the Third Social Communications Day: *AAS* 61 (1969), 456.

contact—through suitable initiatives—with those in charge of the various phases of production and transmission. In this way they will ensure that the fundamental human values that form part of the true good of society are not ignored or deliberately attacked. Rather they will ensure the broadcasting of programmes that present in the right light family problems and their proper solution. In this regard my venerated predecessor Paul VI wrote: "Producers must know and respect the needs of the family, and this sometimes presupposes in them true courage, and always a high sense of responsibility. In fact they are expected to avoid anything that could harm the family in its existence, its stability, its balance and its happiness. Every attack on the fundamental value of the family—meaning eroticism or violence, the defence of divorce or of antisocial attitudes among young people—is an attack on the true good of man".[176]

I myself, on a similar occasion, pointed out that families "to a considerable extent need to be able to count on the good will, integrity and sense of responsibility of the media professionals —publishers, writers, producers, directors, playwrights, newsmen, commentators and actors".[177] It is therefore also the duty of the Church to

[176] *Ibid.*
[177] John Paul II, Message for the 1980 World Social Communications Day: *Insegnamenti di Giovanni Paolo II*, III, 1 (1980), 1044.

144

continue to devote every care to these categories, at the same time encouraging and supporting Catholics who feel the call and have the necessary talents, to take up this sensitive type of work.

IV – PASTORAL CARE OF THE FAMILY IN DIFFICULT CASES

Particular circumstances

77.   An even more generous, intelligent and prudent pastoral commitment, modelled on the Good Shepherd, is called for in the case of families which, often independently of their own wishes and through pressures of various other kinds, find themselves faced by situations which are objectively difficult.

In this regard it is necessary to call special attention to certain particular groups which are more in need not only of assistance but also of more incisive action upon public opinion and especially upon cultural, economic and juridical structures, in order that the profound causes of their needs may be eliminated as far as possible.

Such for example are the families of migrant workers; the families of those obliged to be away for long periods, such as members of the armed forces, sailors and all kinds of itinerant people; the families of those in prison, of refugees and exiles; the families in big cities living practically speaking as outcasts; families with no home; incomplete or single-parent families; families with children that are handicapped or addicted to drugs; the families of alcoholics; families that have been uprooted from their cultural and social environment or are in danger of losing it; families discriminated against for political or other reasons; families that are ideologically divided; families that are unable to make ready contact with the parish; families experiencing violence or unjust treatment because of their faith; teenage married couples; the elderly, who are often obliged to live alone with inadequate means of subsistence.

The families of migrants, especially in the case of manual workers and farm workers, should be able to find a homeland everywhere in the Church. This is a task stemming from the nature of the Church, as being the sign of unity in diversity. As far as possible these people should be looked after by priests of their own rite, culture and language. It is also the Church's task to appeal to the public conscience and to all those in authority in social, economic and political life, in order that workers may find employment in their own regions and homelands, that they may receive just wages, that their families may be reunited as soon as possible, be respected in their cultural identity and treated on an equal footing with others, and that their children may be given the chance to learn a trade and exercise it, as also the chance to own the land needed for working and living.

A difficult problem is that of the family which

is *ideologically divided*. In these cases particular pastoral care is needed. In the first place it is necessary to maintain tactful personal contact with such families. The believing members must be strengthened in their faith and supported in their Christian lives. Although the party faithful to Catholicism cannot give way, dialogue with the other party must always be kept alive. Love and respect must be freely shown, in the firm hope that unity will be maintained. Much also depends on the relationship between parents and children. Moreover, ideologies which are alien to the faith can stimulate the believing members of the family to grow in faith and in the witness of love.

Other difficult circumstances in which the family needs the help of the ecclesial community and its pastors are: the children's adolescence, which can be disturbed, rebellious and sometimes stormy; the children's marriage, which takes them away from their family; lack of understanding or lack of love on the part of those held most dear; abandonment by one of the spouses, or his or her death, which brings the painful experience of widowhood, or the death of a family member, which breaks up and deeply transforms the original family nucleus.

Similarly, the Church cannot ignore the time of old age, with all its positive and negative aspects. In old age married love, which has been increasingly purified and ennobled by long and unbroken fidelity, can be deepened. There is the opportunity of offering to others, in a new form, the kindness and the wisdom gathered over the years, and what energies remain. But there is also the burden of loneliness, more often psychological and emotional rather than physical, which results from abandonment or neglect on the part of children and relations. There is also suffering caused by ill-health, by the gradual loss of strength, by the humiliation of having to depend on others, by the sorrow of feeling that one is perhaps a burden to one's loved ones, and by the approach of the end of life. These are the circumstances in which, as the Synod Fathers suggested, it is easier to help people understand and live the lofty aspects of the spirituality of marriage and the family, aspects which take their inspiration from the value of Christ's Cross and Resurrection, the source of sanctification and profound happiness in daily life, in the light of the great eschatological realities of eternal life.

In all these different situations let prayer, the source of light and strength and the nourishment of Christian hope, never be neglected.

Mixed marriages

78. The growing number of mixed marriages between Catholics and other baptized persons also calls for special pastoral attention in the light of the directives and norms contained in the most recent documents of the Holy See and in those drawn up by the Episcopal Conferences, in order

to permit their practical application to the various situations.

Couples living in a mixed marriage have special needs, which can be put under three main headings.

In the first place, attention must be paid to the obligations that faith imposes on the Catholic party with regard to the free exercise of the faith and the consequent obligation to ensure, as far as is possible, the Baptism and upbringing of the children in the Catholic faith.[178]

There must be borne in mind the particular difficulties inherent in the relationships between husband and wife with regard to respect for religious freedom: this freedom could be violated either by undue pressure to make the partner change his or her beliefs, for by placing obstacles in the way of the free manifestation of these beliefs by religious practice.

With regard to the liturgical and canonical form of marriage, Ordinaries can make wide use of their faculties to meet various necessities.

In dealing with these special needs, the following points should be kept in mind:

— In the appropriate preparation for this type of marriage, every reasonable effort must be made to ensure a proper understanding of

[178] Cf. Paul VI, Motu Proprio *Matrimonia Mixta*, 4-5: *AAS* 62 (1970), 257-259; John Paul II, Address to the participants in the plenary meeting of the Secretariat for Promoting Christian Unity (13 November 1981): *L'Osservatore Romano*, 14 November 1981.

Catholic teaching on the qualities and obligations of marriage, and also to ensure that the pressures and obstacles mentioned above will not occur.

— It is of the greatest importance that, through the support of the community, the Catholic party should be strengthened in faith and positively helped to mature in understanding and practising that faith, so as to become a credible witness within the family through his or her own life and through the quality of love shown to the other spouse and the children.

Marriages between Catholics and other baptized persons have their own particular nature, but they contain numerous elements that could well be made good use of and developed, both for their intrinsic value and for the contribution that they can make to the ecumenical movement. This is particularly true when both parties are faithful to their religious duties. Their common Baptism and the dynamism of grace provide the spouses in these marriages with the basis and motivation for expressing their unity in the sphere of moral and spiritual values.

For this purpose, and also in order to highlight the ecumenical importance of mixed marriages which are fully lived in the faith of the two Christian spouses, an effort should be made to establish cordial cooperation between the Catholic and the non-Catholic ministers from the time that preparations begin for the marriage and the wedding ceremony, even though this does not always prove easy.

With regard to the sharing of the non-Catholic party in Eucharistic Communion, the norms issued by the Secretariat for Promoting Christian Unity should be followed.[179]

Today in many parts of the world marriages between Catholics and non-baptized persons are growing in numbers. In many such marriages the non-baptized partner professes another religion, and his beliefs are to be treated with respect, in accordance with the principles set out in the Second Vatican Council's Declaration *Nostra Aetate* on relations with non-Christian religions. But in many other such marriages, particularly in secularized societies, the non-baptized person professes no religion at all. In these marriages there is a need for Episcopal Conferences and for individual Bishops to ensure that there are proper pastoral safeguards for the faith of the Catholic partner and for the free exercise of his faith, above all in regard to his duty to do all in his power to ensure the Catholic baptism and education of the children of the marriage. Likewise the Catholic must be assisted in every possible way to offer within his family a genuine witness to the Catholic faith and to Catholic life.

---

[179] Instruction *In Quibus Rerum Circumstantiis* (15 June 1972): *AAS* 64 (1972), 518-525; Note of 17 October 1973: *AAS* 65 (1973), 616-619.

79.   In its solicitude to protect the family in all its dimensions, not only the religious one, the Synod of Bishops did not fail to take into careful consideration certain situations which are irregular in a religious sense and often in the civil sense too. Such situations, as a result to today's rapid cultural changes, are unfortunately becoming widespread also among Catholics, with no little damage to the very institution of the family and to society, of which the family constitutes the basic cell.

a) *Trial marriages*

80.   A first example of an irregular situation is provided by what are called "trial marriages", which many people today would like to justify by attributing a certain value to them. But human reason leads one to see that they are unacceptable, by showing the unconvincing nature of carrying out an "experiment" with human beings, whose dignity demands that they should be always and solely the term of a self-giving love without limitations of time or of any other circumstance.

The Church, for her part, cannot admit such a kind of union, for further and original reasons which derive from faith. For, in the first place, the gift of the body in the sexual relationship is a real symbol of the giving of the whole person: such a giving, moreover, in the present state of

152

things cannot take place with full truth without the concourse of the love of charity, given by Christ. In the second place, marriage between two baptized persons is a real symbol of the union of Christ and the Church, which is not a temporary or "trial" union but one which is eternally faithful. Therefore between two baptized persons there can exist only an indissoluble marriage.

Such a situation cannot usually be overcome unless the human person, from childhood, with the help of Christ's grace and without fear, has been trained to dominate concupiscence from the beginning and to establish relationships of genuine love with other people. This cannot be secured without a true education in genuine love and in the right use of sexuality, such as to introduce the human person in every aspect, and therefore the bodily aspect too, into the fullness of the mystery of Christ.

It will be very useful to investigate the causes of this phenomenon, including its psychological and sociological aspect, in order to find the proper remedy.

b) *De facto free unions*

81.   This means unions without any publicly recognized institutional bond, either civil or religious.   This phenomenon, which is becoming ever more frequent, cannot fail to concern pastors of souls, also because it may be based on widely varying factors, the consequences of

which may perhaps be containable by suitable action.

Some people consider themselves almost forced into a free union by difficult economic, cultural or religious situations, on the grounds that, if they contracted a regular marriage, they would be exposed to some form of harm, would lose economic advantages, would be discriminated against, etc. In other cases, however, one encounters people who scorn, rebel against or reject society, the institution of the family and the social and political order, or who are solely seeking pleasure. Then there are those who are driven to such situations by extreme ignorance or poverty, sometimes by a conditioning due to situations of real injustice, or by a certain psychological immaturity that makes them uncertain or afraid to enter into a stable and definitive union. In some countries, traditional customs presume that the true and proper marriage will take place only after a period of cohabitation and the birth of the first child.

Each of these elements presents the Church with arduous pastoral problems, by reason of the serious consequences deriving from them, both religious and moral (the loss of the religious sense of marriage seen in the light of the Covenant of God with his people; deprivation of the grace of the sacrament; grave scandal), and also social consequences (the destruction of the concept of the family; the weakening of the sense of fidelity, also towards society; possible psychological dam-

154

age to the children; the strengthening of selfishness).

The pastors and the ecclesial community should take care to become acquainted with such situations and their actual causes, case by case. They should make tactful and respectful contact with the couples concerned, and enlighten them patiently, correct them charitably and show them the witness of Christian family life, in such a way as to smooth the path for them to regularize their situation. But above all there must be a campaign of prevention, by fostering the sense of fidelity in the whole moral and religious training of the young, instructing them concerning the conditions and structures that favour such fidelity, without which there is no true freedom; they must be helped to reach spiritual maturity and enabled to understand the rich human and supernatural reality of marriage as a sacrament.

The People of God should also make approaches to the public authorities, in order that the latter may resist these tendencies which divide society and are harmful to the dignity, security and welfare of the citizens as individuals, and they must try to ensure that public opinion is not led to undervalue the institutional importance of marriage and the family. And since in many regions young people are unable to get married properly because of extreme poverty deriving from unjust or inadequate social and economic structures, society and the public authorities should favour legitimate marriage by means of a series of social and political actions which will guarantee a family wage, by issuing directives ensuring housing fitting for family life and by creating opportunities for work and life.

c) *Catholics in civil marriages*

82.   There are increasing cases of Catholics who, for ideological or practical reasons, prefer to contract a merely civil marriage, and who reject or at least defer religious marriage. Their situation cannot of course be likened to that of people simply living together without any bond at all, because in the present case there is at least a certain commitment to a properly-defined and probably stable state of life, even though the possibility of a future divorce is often present in the minds of those entering a civil marriage. By seeking public recognition of their bond on the part of the State, such couples show that they are ready to accept not only its advantages but also its obligations. Nevertheless, not even this situation is acceptable to the Church.

The aim of pastoral action will be to make these people understand the need for consistency between their choice of life and the faith that they profess, and to try to do everything possible to induce them to regularize their situation in the light of Christian principles. While treating them with great charity and bringing them into the life of the respective communities, the pastors of the Church will regrettably not be able to admit them to the sacraments.

d) *Separated or divorced persons who have not remarried*

83.   Various reasons can unfortunately lead to the often irreparable breakdown of valid marriages. These include mutual lack of understanding and the inability to enter into interpersonal relationships. Obviously, separation must be considered as a last resort, after all other reasonable attempts at reconciliation have proved vain.

Loneliness and other difficulties are often the lot of separated spouses, especially when they are the innocent parties. The ecclesial community must support such people more than ever. It must give them much respect, solidarity, understanding and practical help, so that they can preserve their fidelity even in their difficult situation; and it must help them to cultivate the need to forgive which is inherent in Christian love, and to be ready perhaps to return to their former married life.

The situation is similar for people who have undergone divorce, but, being well aware that the valid marriage bond is indissoluble, refrain from becoming involved in a new union and devote themselves solely to carrying out their family duties and the responsibilities of Christian life. In such cases their example of fidelity and Christian consistency takes on particular value as a witness before the world and the Church. Here it is even more necessary for the Church to offer continual love and assistance, without there being any obstacle to admission to the sacraments.

e) *Divorced persons who have remarried*

84.   Daily experience unfortunately shows that people who have obtained a divorce usually intend to enter into a new union, obviously not with a Catholic religious ceremony. Since this is an evil that, like the others, is affecting more and more Catholics as well, the problem must be faced with resolution and without delay. The Synod Fathers studied it expressly. The Church, which was set up to lead to salvation all people and especially the baptized, cannot abandon to their own devices those who have been previously bound by sacramental marriage and who have attempted a second marriage. The Church will therefore make untiring efforts to put at their disposal her means of salvation.

Pastors must know that, for the sake of truth, they are obliged to exercise careful discernment of situations. There is in fact a difference between those who have sincerely tried to save their first marriage and have been unjustly abandoned, and those who through their own grave fault have destroyed a canonically valid marriage. Finally, there are those who have entered into a second union for the sake of the children's upbringing, and who are sometimes subjectively certain in conscience that their previous and irreparably destroyed marriage had never been valid.

Together with the Synod, I earnestly call upon pastors and the whole community of the faithful to help the divorced, and with solicitous care to make sure that they do not consider themselves as separated from the Church, for as baptized persons they can, and indeed must, share in her life. They should be encouraged to listen to the word of God, to attend the Sacrifice of the Mass, to persevere in prayer, to contribute to works of charity and to community efforts in favour of justice, to bring up their children in the Christian faith, to cultivate the spirit and practice of penance and thus implore, day by day, God's grace. Let the Church pray for them, encourage them and show herself a merciful mother, and thus sustain them in faith and hope.

However, the Church reaffirms her practice, which is based upon Sacred Scripture, of not admitting to Eucharistic Communion divorced persons who have remarried. They are unable to be admitted thereto from the fact that their state and condition of life objectively contradict that union of love between Christ and the Church which is signified and effected by the Eucharist. Besides this, there is another special pastoral reason: if these people were admitted to the Eucharist, the faithful would be led into error and confusion regarding the Church's teaching about the indissolubility of marriage.

Reconciliation in the sacrament of Penance, which would open the way to the Eucharist, can only be granted to those who, repenting of having broken the sign of the Covenant and of fidelity to Christ, are sincerely ready to undertake a way of life that is no longer in contradiction to the indissolubility of marriage. This means, in practice, that when, for serious reasons such as for example the children's upbringing, a man and a woman cannot satisfy the obligation to separate, they "take on themselves the duty to live in complete continence, that is, by abstinence from the acts proper to married couples".[180]

Similarly, the respect due to the sacrament of Matrimony, to the couples themselves and their families, and also to the community of the faithful, forbids any pastor, for whatever reason or pretext even of a pastoral nature, to perform ceremonies of any kind for divorced people who remarry. Such ceremonies would give the impression of the celebration of a new sacramentally valid marriage, and would thus lead people into error concerning the indissolubility of a validly contracted marriage.

[180] John Paul II, Homily at the close of the Sixth Synod of Bishops, 7 (25 October 1980): *AAS* 72 (1980), 1082.

By acting in this way, the Church professes her own fidelity to Christ and to his truth. At the same time she shows motherly concern for these children of hers, especially those who, through no fault of their own, have been abandoned by their legitimate partner.

With firm confidence she believes that those who have rejected the Lord's command and are still living in this state will be able to obtain from God the grace of conversion and salvation, provided that they have persevered in prayer, penance and charity.

Those without a family

85. I wish to add a further word for a category of people whom, as a result of the actual circumstances in which they are living, and this often not through their own deliberate wish, I consider particularly close to the Heart of Christ and deserving of the affection and active solicitude of the Church and of pastors.

There exist in the world countless people who unfortunately cannot in any sense claim membership of what could be called in the proper sense a family. Large sections of humanity live in conditions of extreme poverty, in which promiscuity, lack of housing, the irregular nature and instability of relationships and the extreme lack of education make it impossible in practice to speak of a true family. There are

161

others who, for various reasons, have been left alone in the world. And yet for all of these people there exists a "good news of the family".

On behalf of those living in extreme poverty, I have already spoken of the urgent need to work courageously in order to find solutions, also at the political level, which will make it possible to help them and to overcome this inhuman condition of degradation.

It is a task that faces the whole of society but in a special way the authorities, by reason of their position and the responsibilities flowing therefrom, and also families, which must show great understanding and willingness to help.

For those who have no natural family the doors of the great family which is the Church —the Church which finds concrete expression in the diocesan and the parish family, in ecclesial basic communities and in movements of the apostolate—must be opened even wider. No one is without a family in this world: the Church is a home and family for everyone, especially those who "labour and are heavy laden".[181]

[181] *Mt* 11:28.

CONCLUSION

86.   At the end of this Apostolic Exhortation my thoughts turn with earnest solicitude:

to you, married couples, to you, fathers and mothers of families;

to you, young men and women, the future and the hope of the Church and the world, destined to be the dynamic central nucleus of the family in the approaching third millennium;

to you, venerable and dear Brothers in the Episcopate and in the priesthood, beloved sons and daughters in the religious life, souls consecrated to the Lord, who bear witness before married couples to the ultimate reality of the love of God;

to you, upright men and women, who for any reason whatever give thought to the fate of the family.

The future of humanity passes by way of the family.

It is therefore indispensable and urgent that every person of good will should endeavour to save and foster the values and requirements of the family.

I feel that I must ask for a particular effort in this field from the sons and daughters of the

Church. Faith gives them full knowledge of God's wonderful plan: they therefore have an extra reason for caring for the reality that is the family in this time of trial and of grace.

They must *show the family special love.* This is an injunction that calls for concrete action.

Loving the family means being able to appreciate its values and capabilities, fostering them always. Loving the family means identifying the dangers and the evils that menace it, in order to overcome them. Loving the family means endeavouring to create for it an environment favourable for its development. The modern Christian family is often tempted to be discouraged and is distressed at the growth of its difficulties; it is an eminent form of love to give it back its reasons for confidence in itself, in the riches that it possesses by nature and grace, and in the mission that God has entrusted to it. "Yes indeed, the families of today must be called back to their original position. They must follow Christ ".[182]

Christians also have the mission of *proclaiming with joy and conviction the Good News about the family,* for the family absolutely needs to hear ever anew and to understand ever more deeply the authentic words that reveal its identity, its inner resources and the importance of its mission in the City of God and in that of man.

The Church knows the path by which the

[182] John Paul II, Letter *Appropinquat Iam* (15 August 1980), 1: *AAS* 72 (1980), 791.

164

family can reach the heart of the deepest truth about itself. The Church has learned this path at the school of Christ and the school of history interpreted in the light of the Spirit. She does not impose it but she feels an urgent need to propose it to everyone without fear and indeed with great confidence and hope, although she knows that the Good News includes the subject of the Cross. But it is through the Cross that the family can attain the fullness of its being and the perfection of its love.

Finally, I wish to call on all Christians to *collaborate cordially and courageously* with all people of good will who are serving the family in accordance with their responsibilities. The individuals and groups, movements and associations in the Church which devote themselves to the family's welfare, acting in the Church's name and under her inspiration, often find themselves side by side with other individuals and institutions working for the same ideal. With faithfulness to the values of the Gospel and of the human person and with respect for lawful pluralism in initiatives this collaboration can favour a more rapid and integral advancement of the family.

And now, at the end of my pastoral message, which is intended to draw everyone's attention to the demanding yet fascinating roles of the Christian family, I wish to invoke the protection of the Holy Family of Nazareth.

Through God's mysterious design, it was in that family that the Son of God spent long years of a hidden life. It is therefore the prototype and example for all Christian families. It was unique in the world. Its life was passed in anonymity and silence in a little town in Palestine. It underwent trials of poverty, persecution and exile. It glorified God in an incomparably exalted and pure way. And it will not fail to help Christian families—indeed, all the families in the world—to be faithful to their day-to-day duties, to bear the cares and tribulations of life, to be open and generous to the needs of others, and to fulfil with joy the plan of God in their regard.

Saint Joseph was "a just man", a tireless worker, the upright guardian of those entrusted to his care. May he always guard, protect and enlighten families.

May the Virgin Mary, who is the Mother of the Church, also be the Mother of "the Church of the home". Thanks to her motherly aid, may each Christian family really become a "little Church" in which the mystery of the Church of Christ is mirrored and given new life. May she, the Handmaid of the Lord, be an example of humble and generous acceptance of the will of God. May she, the Sorrowful Mother at the foot of the Cross, comfort the sufferings and dry the tears of those in distress because of the difficulties of their families.

May Christ the Lord, the Universal King, the King of Families, be present in every Christian home as he was at Cana, bestowing light, joy, serenity and strength. On the solemn day dedicated to his Kingship I beg of him that every family may generously make its own contribution to the coming of his Kingdom in the world—"a kingdom of truth and life, a kingdom of holiness and grace, a kingdom of justice, love, and peace",[183] towards which history is journeying.

I entrust each family to him, to Mary, and to Joseph. To their hands and their hearts I offer this Exhortation: may it be they who present it to you, venerable Brothers and beloved sons and daughters, and may it be they who open your hearts to the light that the Gospel sheds on every family.

I assure you all of my constant prayers and I cordially impart the Apostolic Blessing to each and every one of you, in the name of the Father, and of the Son, and of the Holy Spirit.

Given in Rome, at Saint Peter's, on the twenty-second day of November, the Solemnity of Our Lord Jesus Christ, Universal King, in the year 1981, the fourth of the Pontificate.

Joannes Paulus pp. II

---

[183] The Roman Missal, Preface of Christ the King.

CONTENTS

INTRODUCTION

1. The Church at the service of the family . . 3
2. The Synod of 1980 in continuity with preceding Synods 4
3. The precious value of marriage and of the
   family 5

PART ONE

BRIGHT SPOTS AND SHADOWS
FOR THE FAMILY TODAY

4. The need to understand the situation . . . 8
5. Evangelical discernment 9
6. The situation of the family in the world today 12
7. The influence of circumstances on the consciences of the faithful 14
8. Our age needs wisdom 14
9. Gradualness and conversion 16
10. Inculturation 17

PART TWO

THE PLAN OF GOD
FOR MARRIAGE AND THE FAMILY

11. Man, the image of the God who is love . . 19
12. Marriage and communion between God and
    people 21
13. Jesus Christ, Bridegroom of the Church, and
    the sacrament of Matrimony 22

14. Children, the precious gift of marriage . . 26
15. The family, a communion of persons . . . 27
16. Marriage and virginity or celibacy 28

PART THREE

THE ROLE
OF THE CHRISTIAN FAMILY

17. Family, become what you are 32

I – FORMING A COMMUNITY OF PERSONS

18. Love as the principle and power of com-
    munion 34
19. The indivisible unity of conjugal communion 35
20. An indissoluble communion 37
21. The broader communion of the family . . 39
22. The rights and role of women 42
23. Women and society 44
24. Offences against women's dignity 46
25. Men as husbands and fathers 47
26. The rights of children 49
27. The elderly in the family 51

II – SERVING LIFE

1) *The transmission of life*

28. Cooperators in the love of God the Creator 53
29. The Church's teaching and norm, always old
    yet always new 54
30. The Church stands for life 55
31. That God's design may be ever more com-
    pletely fulfilled 58
32. In an integral vision of the human person
    and of his or her vocation 59

33. The Church as Teacher and Mother for couples in difficulty 62
34. The moral progress of married people . . . 66
35. Instilling conviction and offering practical help 69

2) *Education*

36. The right and duty of parents regarding education 70
37. Educating in the essential values of human life 72
38. The mission to educate and the sacrament of marriage 74
39. First experience of the Church 76
40. Relations with other educating agents . . . 78
41. Manifold service to life 80

III – PARTICIPATING
IN THE DEVELOPMENT OF SOCIETY

42. The family as the first and vital cell of society 81
43. Family life as an experience of communion and sharing 82
44. The social and political role 84
45. Society at the service of the family 85
46. The charter of family rights 86
47. The Christian family's grace and responsibility 89
48. For a new international order 90

IV – SHARING IN THE LIFE AND MISSION
OF THE CHURCH

49. The family, within the mystery of the Church 91
50. A specific and original ecclesial role . . . 93

1) *The Christian family as a believing and evangelizing community*

51. Faith as the discovery and admiring awareness of God's plan for the family 95

173

52. The Christian family's ministry of evangeli-
    zation   97
53. Ecclesial service   99
54. To preach the Gospel to the whole creation   100

  2) *The Christian family as a community in
     dialogue with God*

55. The Church's sanctuary in the home . . .   102
56. Marriage as a sacrament of mutual sanctifica-
    tion and an act of worship   103
57. Marriage and the Eucharist   105
58. The sacrament of conversion and reconciliation   107
59. Family prayer   108
60. Educators in prayer   109
61. Liturgical prayer and private prayer . . .   111
62. Prayer and life   113

  3) *The Christian family as a community at
     the service of man*

63. The new commandment of love   114
64. To discover the image of God in each brother
    and sister   116

PART FOUR

PASTORAL CARE OF THE FAMILY:
STAGES, STRUCTURES, AGENTS
AND SITUATIONS

I – STAGES OF PASTORAL CARE
OF THE FAMILY

65. The Church accompanies the Christian family
    on its journey through life   119
66. Preparation for marriage   120
67. The celebration   125

68. Celebration of marriage and evangelization of
    non-believing baptized persons 127
69. Pastoral care after marriage 130

II – Structures
of family pastoral care

70. The ecclesial community and in particular
    the parish 132
71. The family 133
72. Associations of families for families . . . 135

III – Agents of the pastoral care
of the family

73. Bishops and priests 137
74. Men and women religious 139
75. Lay specialists 141
76. Recipients and agents of social communications 142

IV – Pastoral care of the family
in difficult cases

77. Particular circumstances 145
78. Mixed marriages 148
79. Pastoral action in certain irregular situations 152
80. a) *Trial marriages* 152
81. b) *De facto free unions* 153
82. c) *Catholics in civil marriages* 156
83. d) *Separated or divorced persons who have
    not remarried* 157
84. e) *Divorced persons who have remarried* . . 158
85. Those without a family 161

86. Conclusion 163